GOD DOESN'T HAVE BAD HAIR DAYS

GOD

DOESN'T HAVE
BAD HAIR DAYS

Ten Spiritual Experiments that Will Bring More
Abundance, Joy, and Love to Your Life

by PAM GROUT

RUNNING PRESS
PHILADELPHIA · LONDON

Printed in Canada

9   8   7   6   5   4   3   2   1
Digit on the right indicates the number of this printing

Library of Congress Control Number: 2005901968

ISBN-13: 978-0-7624-2439-9
ISBN-10: 0-7624-2439-7

Cover illustration by Alex Gross
Cover design by Matthew Goodman
Interior design by Matthew Goodman
Edited by Jennifer Kasius

This book may be ordered by mail from the publisher.
Please include $2.50 for postage and handling.
But try your bookstore first!

Running Press Book Publishers
125 South Twenty-second Street
Philadelphia, Pennsylvania 19103-4399

Visit us on the web!
www.runningpress.com

THIS BOOK IS DEDICATED TO
Dennis Kucinich and every other human being who believes a
better world is not only possible, but can feel it gathering breath.

SHOUT OUTS

Like winning a Superbowl or building a pyramid, writing a book is a team effort.
I'd like to thank the follow members of Team Hair Days:

THE FRONT LINE:

Susan Schulman, the agent who said, "Yes, this idea is a winner, run with it."
Matthew Carnicelli, my agent who took the ball and did.
Jennifer Kasius, my editor at Running Press, who caught
that ball and knew what to do with it.

THE MIDDLE LINEBACKERS :

Wendy Druen, Betty and Harry Shaffer, Bob Savino (whose words, by
the way, are far more eloquent and profound than mine ever will be),
Diane Silver, Victoria Moran, Ivy Rue, Ennola Charity, Andrea Hoag, and Stan Russell.

THE HOME TEAM:

Jim Dick, who fed me, rubbed my back,
and made sure my daughter got picked up from school.
Trivia Quantum Morpheus Mr. Norris X-Cat Grout whose strolls on the computer keys
(FFFRJRIFJJ) didn't make much sense, but helped keep things in perspective.
Tasman Grout, who will always be the inspiration for any project I undertake.

"My fingers are being pried off all I think I know. Certainty is very useful, but it can really close your mind off to the true light."

—David O. Russell, filmmaker

"Don't face reality. Create Reality."

CONTENTS

INTRODUCTION

"What's your persuasion on the big guy, kid?"
—Tom Hanks in *Polar Express*

Two months before I turned 35, my boyfriend of several years dumped me for a twenty-something, bleached-blonde law student. To say I was devastated would be a gross understatement. Keep in mind that this was about the same time the single woman/ asteroid study came out. You know the one I'm talking about? The one that publicly revealed that women over 30 have roughly the same odds of getting married as they do of being sideswiped by an asteroid.

After several days of lying in bed and staring at my ceiling fan, I finally came to the conclusion that I had two choices left. I could either slit my veins in a warm bath or sign up for a month-long work-study program at Esalen, the self-improvement mecca in California. Knowing how my roomate at the time despised messes, I opted for Esalan.

On the second night there, I met a handsome former surfer named Stan who convinced me to spend the evening with him listening to the Pacific Ocean crashing against the Big Sur cliffs. We accidentally fell asleep in one of the massage rooms huddled together to stay warm. Not that it worked. April winds off the Pacific can be ferocious and even with our combined body heat, we practically froze to death.

If Stan hadn't been so cute and I hadn't been so desperate to get over the jerk who tossed me aside like some used bag of Doritos, I probably would have excused myself and gone back to my insulated sleeping bag. But I stayed until the next morning when "the dawn's early light" revealed that there was a space heater next to the mat where we lay the whole time. A space heater that we could have turned on and used to keep warm!!

In a nutshell, that's what this book is about. There's a space heater or rather an energy force that's right inside us and we haven't bothered to turn it on. Instead, we lay here freezing, unhappy, and believing there's nothing we can do about our sad, desperate lives. Most of us are totally oblivious to the fact that the space heater even exists. We think of life as a random crapshoot and believe we don't have a lot of control over what happens. C'est la vie.

Those of us who do know about the space heater (i.e. the internal energy source that could totally heat us up, make us happy, and give us meaningful lives) don't understand how it works. We've heard rumors that praying turns it on, that good work keeps it going, but nobody seems to know for sure. This religion tells us to tithe. That one suggests meditation. The next one convinces us to give up our earthly belongings and trek to the Himalayas. So which is it? Is God really that vague and mysterious? And why does the spiritual force only work sometimes? God at best is finicky and fickle, certainly nothing you can bank on.

Or is he? What I'd like to suggest is that God—or what I'm calling spiritual energy—is 100 percent reliable. It works every time like a math principle or Newton's Second Law of Physics. Two plus two always equals four. Blue and yellow mixed together always make green. Balls dropped off roofs always fall. Thoughts and consciousness always create matter.

FIRST TIME, EVERY TIME

"Everyone who is seriously involved in the pursuit of science becomes
convinced that a spirit is manifest in the laws of the universe—a
spirit vastly superior to that of man."

—Albert Einstein

When a kindergartner bails off the monkey bars, the principle of gravity works even though he has no clue what gravity is or even how to pronounce it. Likewise, spiritual principles are at work in your life whether you understand them, can pronounce them, or even want them.

Take a standard 8-½ by 11-inch piece of paper. Drop it from shoulder level. Most likely, it fell to the ground. But if you take that same piece of paper, fold it just right, add a paper clip to the bottom, you can sail it all the way across your average Burger King.

The paper still weighs the same. It's still the same color, the same texture. But by applying the principles of velocity, force, and lift, you make what used to be an "impossible thing" possible.

Seven hundred thousand pound planes now fly through the air, not because we changed the law of gravity, but because Wilbur and Orville Wright learned higher laws that transcend it.

By learning and applying spiritual laws, you too can transcend anything. In this book, you'll discover that the world operates according to universal spiritual principles that, like gravity, influence your life at every moment. And here's the kicker. These spiritual principles are more profound than physical laws and affect your life whether you're aware of their existence or not.

By becoming aware of these laws and utilizing them in your favor, you can fling wide the doors of creativity, love, and joy. Any light bulb with a working filament and an electric current has the potential to light up a room. It doesn't matter whether that light bulb is big or small, round or square, yellow or white. It doesn't matter where it's been or how it was used in the past. If a light is plugged to its source, it's going to dispense light.

Through the conscious and deliberate approach to spirituality presented in this book, you'll learn how to stay plugged in to your source and how to dramatically improve every area of your life.

A QUICK NOTE FROM OUR SPONSOR

"In my head, God has dark red hair and a beard. He doesn't wear clothes, but it's okay, because you can't see below his shoulders anyway. Everything else is always covered by clouds."

—Laura Moriarty, *The Center of Everything*

God, Schmod. All you have to do is drive through East L.A. or read about Sudan to realize that God is a bunch of hooey. The guy couldn't possibly exist. Or if he does, he's got to be some kind of evil sadist. The guy's worse than an absentee landlord.

Glad we got that over with. Ready to hear my side?

The God addressed in this book is pure, inexorable light—the void that makes up the universe. Matter, as scientists have proven by breaking it down and putting it into a particle accelerator, is mostly empty space. According to the British physicist Sir Arthur Eddington, "Matter is 99.9999999 percent ghostly nothingness, to be precise."

In physics, light is the only absolute. It lies beyond the material world of matter, shape, and form. It fills the cosmos, saturates reality, and supersedes time and space.

That's what I mean by God. An absolute pure light that, like water, runs into any opening it is given.

Think of a mountain cabin that has been boarded up all winter. The minute you open the doors and windows, light streams in of its own accord. You don't have to plead or beg. Light can never be less than light.

We shape the light by our consciousness. For some, it's helpful to shape God into a father. Into a loving "him." There's nothing wrong with that if it's useful. I will probably call the force a "him" myself at some point in this book. Old habits die hard.

Another popular shape for God is "love." When we chose love—or allow our minds to be one with love, life is wonderful. When we turn away from love, pain sets in. It's a mental choice we make every day.

The form this all-powerful, all-creative, all-loving potential takes in and through you depends on your consciousness, the energy behind your intent. When Jesus talked about finding heaven, he was not talking about winning doggy points or some place up in the sky. The Aramaic translation of heaven is expansion. Finding "heaven" is finding the expanding potential, the ultimate Truth within the light. This is the truth Jesus said would set us free.

STILL A C-STUDENT

"Life is waiting everywhere, the future is flowering everywhere, but we only see a small part of it and step on much of it with our feet."
—Hermann Hesse, German poet and novelist

If you've been in metaphysical, spiritual circles for any time at all, you already know your thoughts create your reality, that there's a power in the universe that can heal, and that you and you alone design your own life. Unfortunately, there's still this tiny little problem, this one itty-bitty catch.

You don't really believe it.

You think you do. You probably even talk about it with like-minded friends. But I happen to know the truth. If you *really* understood the power of the universe, you'd be fabulously wealthy, ecstatically happy, and so "in love" with your fellow humanoids that it would never occur to you to pick up a book like this.

Quite frankly, I'm glad you did. This little book will prove to you once and for all that there is a force in this universe that has your best interests at heart. This book has ten specific, easy-to-try experiments to prove there's a God.

Only we're not going to call it God. That word has more baggage than the Chicago airport the Sunday after Thanksgiving. Some New Age types prefer the phrase "inner guidance" or the "all there is." You can call it Cosmo Kramer, for all I care, but just like Shakespeare's "rose by any other name," it's the same deal. There's an all-powerful force that thrums through your bones. It's a force you can use to overcome any difficulty, to achieve great success. It's a force whose truth will literally set you free.

It can help you with everything from healing an ulcer to finding a perfect pair of black pumps. Do you need money? Desire a new relationship? Want a more rewarding career? The power I'm talking about can help with all these things. You can even direct this power to provide a vacation to Tahiti.

Take me, for example. A few years ago, I decided to spend a month in Australia. A chiropractor I had a huge crush on had just taken a job there to work with Aborigines. How, I wondered, were we going to fall in love when I was in Kansas and he was 2500 miles away. One look at my bank statement would have convinced any reasonable person that a $1500 plane ticket to Sydney, the going price at that time, was out of the question. But I wanted to go and I was lucky enough to know about the power that could make that happen.

I started planning the trip, began picturing myself romping through the Sydney surf. I mean I got really worked up over this picture in my mind.

Within a week, my editor at *Modern Bride* called.

"I know it's late notice," she began, "But is there any way you'd be willing to go to Australia to write a honeymoon story? We'll pay extra."

"Well, okay," I said. "If you insist."

The force (let's just go ahead and call it Cosmo K since God and his last name Dammit is something usually said when smacking a thumb with a hammer) can literally provide assistance with anything. And the best part is it's available 24/7. I dare you to find me a therapist, a doctor, or even a friend that can make that kind of claim.

You can use Cosmo K to heal and change your body. I was hiking with a friend in the Flatlands near Steamboat Springs, Colorado. Climbing up the one path in the entire park, she tripped over a rock, fell, and her ankle started swelling. I mean, this girl swelled. It wouldn't have been a problem if this had happened next door to a free health clinic, but keep in mind the two of us were 70 minutes (and that's if you walk fast which she couldn't do because she was limping) from the nearest phone, let alone a free health clinic. I told her to direct her body to quit swelling. She started yelling, "Stop swelling. Heal. Stop Swelling. Heal."

"It's okay to say it quietly," I reminded her.

We made it to our camp and she never even had to see a doctor.

It's not lack of talent or potential that has prevented you from turning your life into a masterpiece. It's your refusal to believe, to really, really believe, these laws exist.

COSMO K, BETTER THAN THE ENERGIZER BUNNY

"All life is an experiment. The more experiments you make the better."
–Ralph Waldo Emerson

The ten experiments in this book, each of which take a short 48 hours or less, will prove that the "God power," like electricity, is dependable, predictable, and available to everyone from Saint Francis of Assisi to Barbara Walters. They'll prove what physicists over the past 100 years have discovered—that the force connects all of us and that the reason we control our lives is because every thought we have is an energy wave that affects everything else in the universe.

But, like electricity, you DO have to plug it in. And you do have to quit being so gosh-derned wishy-washy.

Nobody in his or her right mind would call up Sears and say, "Oh just send me something I like." Likewise, you wouldn't call a plumber to fix your toilet and then add, "Just come whenever you feel like it."

Yet that's how most of us practice spirituality. We plead with God on a near-daily basis, but we're wishy-washy, vague, and don't have a clue how spiritual principles work.

God Doesn't Have Bad Hair Days not only explains exactly how spiritual principles work, but it gives concrete instructions for using these principles to better your life.

The catchy title, rather than indicating the God of fundamentalist lore indicates God as a spiritual concept, a positive life force that when tapped and mined sends our lives spinning in unimaginably exciting new directions. The experiments, each of which can be conducted with absolutely no money and very little time expenditure, will prove the following spiritual principles:

1. THE DUDE ABIDES PRINCIPLE.

This is the basic principle, the foundation upon which all the others rest. Basically what it says is, "There is a mind-boggling force that offers infinite love, tolerance, compassion, generosity, beauty, gentleness, joy, peace, and wisdom. And it's yours for the asking. Anytime, anywhere."

The experiment could best be described as an ultimatum. You're going to give the force exactly 48 hours to make its presence known. You're going to demand a clear, unmistakable sign, something that cannot be written off as coincidence.

2. THE VOLKSWAGEN JETTA PRINCIPLE.

Remember that new car you bought a few years ago? When you first decided it was the car of your dreams, it seemed like a really unique car. You figured you'd be the only one in town to proudly drive one. Well, by the time you finally got to the car dealership, read up on it in *Consumer Reports*, and decided on the price you needed to offer, you noticed that practically every eighth car was a

Volkswagen Jetta or whatever car it was you wanted. And that's what happens when you begin to think about something—you start to draw it into your life.

This principle states that "Whatever you Focus on Expands" and to prove it we'll set a clear intention: "This is what I want to see in the next 48 hours." You'll be amazed at all the butterflies, green cars, and nice people running around in the world.

3. THE ALBY EINSTEIN PRINCIPLE.

Even though this principle, "You are a field of energy in an even bigger field of energy," is one of the cornerstone spiritual principles (remember spiritual just means the opposite of material), it actually first came to light, not in a church, but in a physics lab. Yes, it was scientists who first discovered that, despite all appearances to the contrary, human beings are not matter, but continually moving waves of energy.

Other than experiment #9, that proves the Harry Houdini Principle, this is the only experiment that involves equipment, specially-designed, perfectly-tuned equipment. Okay, so it's a metal coat hanger (a specimen of which I'm assuming, unless you're a complete and total slob, is available for use in your closet) and a drinking straw, something you can easily score free of charge at any McDonald's.

4. THE DONALD TRUMP PRINCIPLE.

This principle states "The universe is limitless, abundant, and strangely accommo-dating" and to prove it, we're going to hold Cosmo K to that guarantee he made in the New Testament. Remember that promise that if we'd just let him, he'd clothe us, feed us and take better care of us than the lilies of the valley? Well, for the next 48 hours, we're going to leave our wallets at home. And, yes, that means credit cards, too.

5. THE ABRACADABRA PRINCIPLE.

Most people associate the word abracadabra with magicians pulling rabbits out of hats. It's actually an Aramaic term that translates into English as, "I will create as I speak." It's a powerful concept. It's why Edison often announced the invention of a device before he'd actually invented it. It's why Jim Carrey wrote himself a check for $10 million long before he ever made a movie.

This principle simply says, "Thoughts held in mind create after their kind" and in the experiment you'll discover that all thinking produces form at some level. You'll learn there's no such thing as an idle thought and that all of us are way too cavalier and tolerant of our mind's wandering.

6. THE DEAR ABBY PRINCIPLE.

This principle states that "Cosmo K's loving counsel is ongoing, immediate, and available any time night or day." By realigning your consciousness, you can get answers to every request you ever make. The reason you don't know this is because you've taught yourself the most unnatural habit of being separate, of not communicating with your creator.

In this experiment, we spend 48 hours expecting a specific, concrete answer to a specific, concrete question. But watch out. Last time I tried this, I got fired. In retrospect, it was the perfect answer, maybe the only one I could hear, to the question, "Is it time to launch my freelance writing career?"

7. THE SALLY FIELD PRINCIPLE.

Remember when Sally Field won the Oscar for *Norma Rae*? Clutching that gold statuette with big tears in her eyes, she gushed to the audience as if just figuring it out, "You like me. You really like me!" And that's what this principle clearly states. That dude likes you and wants nothing more than to rain down blessings upon your head.

As you might notice, this is a major departure from what most churches have been preaching for the past 2000 years. As Phineas Parkhurst Quimby, the guy credited with starting the New Thought movement, used to say, "The Christian's God is a tyrant of the worst kind." To effectively work spiritual laws, you have to "get it" deep down in your bones that the God force is unconditional love. Period.

8. THE GODLETS R US PRINCIPLE.

This principle goes something like this: "Anything Jesus, Buddha or Michelle Pfeiffer can do, you can do, too." You know how chicklets grow up to be chickens? And booklets are small-sized books? Well, you're a godlet and, unless I'm under-estimating your power of deduction, I think you know what that means. At this point, most of us suffer from a severe case of arrested development.

I have great sympathy for why some of you have chosen NOT to develop. After all, who wants to be the God most of us believe in. Some guy who lives millions of miles away and stubbornly insists on ignoring everything you ask him to do?

But since you'll soon prove that Cosmo K is the all-loving, creative life force in the universe, you might want to reconsider your inheritance. As the Course in Miracles clearly states, "All your misery comes from the strange belief that you are powerless." In other words, you are not bound by the laws of this world.

9. THE HARRY HOUDINI PRINCIPLE.

This principle states that, "Everything that doesn't look like love is smoke and mirrors." In this experiment, we spend 48 hours examining the premise that we need to be on our guard, that we need to distrust our brothers and sisters. This one, as I mentioned above, requires a prop. Wherever you go for the next 48-hour test period—to the office, the grocery store, the opera—you're required to carry a giant stuffed animal. Don't ask. Just do.

10. THE CHEESE DOES NOT STAND ALONE PRINCIPLE.

This all-important spiritual principle that states that, "Everything I give is given to myself." Oh, I know what you're thinking—that I've either really gone and lost it or I'm a very poor math student. I mean every third-grader knows if you have eight gummy bears and give two away, you're not going to have eight left.

Well, math principles don't work in spiritual law. Spiritual principles are every bit as dependable as math principles, but the principles themselves are often in direct conflict. The world's laws, as I point out in the Donald Trump Principle, are based on scarcity. There's not enough. The laws of the world state that when you give something away, it's gone. You lose. Sorry, Charlie.

Spiritual laws, on the other hand, state that the more you give away, the more you gain. Take love, for example. Give it away and it only grows. Give away joy, peace, or anything that has any real value and you'll get more.

A TRUER, GRANDER VISION

"I have to find it here, right here, bursting uncontainably through the slipshod . . . dragged down dead center of one ordinary life . . . ."
—Bob Savino

When Buckminster Fuller was 32, he made a conscious and deliberate choice to change his life, to find a truer and grander reality. He decided he'd use his own life as an experiment, to see what one penniless, unknown individual might be able to do on behalf of humanity. Dubbing himself Guinea Pig B, he dedicated himself and his consciousness to bringing about change in the world.

At the time he started the experiment, he was what you might call a "nobody." Bankrupt and unemployed, he had a wife and new baby to support. His first child, the new baby's older sister, had just died. He was drinking heavily.

His prospects didn't look promising. But he decided to cast aside the past, to give up limiting thoughts. He wanted to know, "What could one person do to change the world?"

For the next 56 years, he devoted himself to his unique experiment. He took risks. He asked, "What if?"

Not only did he became an architect, an inventor, an author, and a great leader, but between 1927 when he launched the experiment until his death in 1983, he wrote 28 books, received 44 honorary degrees, won 25 U.S. patents, and literally changed the way humans see themselves.

That's what I hope *God Doesn't Have Bad Hair Days* will do for you. I hope it will change the way you see yourself. I hope it will inspire you to conduct an experiment with your own life, to ask, "What is the most I can possibly become?"

Every one of us longs for an extraordinary life, one that sizzles, one that makes others want to stand up and cheer.

I hope you will go out now and become the most fantastic, the most joyful, the most wondrous, the most beautiful, the most tender human being you possibly can.

PART ONE:

THE PRELIMINARIES

"You're being used and you don't even know it. It's time for you to start taking your life back—your real life."

—Gary Renard

Before we get started, I need to ask you a favor. It's a simple favor, won't cost you a penny, and it takes all of three seconds to perform.

Ready?

I'd like you to please rip this page out of the book.

Uh . . . not that I'm all-seeing or anything, but it appears to me that the page I asked you to rip out is still attached.

Why?

Could it be you've been conditioned to believe that "good people" do NOT rip pages out of books? Is it possible you've been taught that books are for reading and that one of your responsibilities, as a good, law-abiding citizen, is to keep your books clean and free from smudges? All I can say is your mother would be proud.

But what I'm also saying is the page I've politely asked you to tear out is of absolutely no value, says nothing of any importance, and is totally and irrefutably irrelevant to the contents of this book.

Except for one thing. It demonstrates a principle this book is going to repeat over and over again. You and all humans like you have learned a lot of lessons in life that are getting in your way. You have picked up a lot of information that doesn't serve you. You're "educated" about a lot of things that aren't true and, in fact, are actually keeping you from becoming all that you are capable of being.

It also demonstrates the one thing that makes this book different than any book you have read before. The message is not in the printed type on these pages. The message is in you. And the only way you're going to get the message is by getting up off your keister and doing the experiments exactly as I instruct you. Now, would you please do me a favor and rip this damned page out of the book.

CHAPTER 1:

"GOD LOOKS LIKE ZZ TOP" AND OTHER ANNOYING MYTHS: WHERE WE LEARN WE ARE BADLY MISINFORMED

"Suppose we've chosen the wrong god. Every time we go to church we're just making him madder and madder."

—Homer Simpson

No sooner did I master my ABC's than I was taught that I, little Pammy Sue Grout, was a miserable sinner and had fallen short of the glory of God. It was a fact same as two plus two equals four and that el-em-in-oh-pee is more than one letter in the alphabetical lineup. The only redeeming part of this all-important lesson is that at least I'm not alone. Turns out, everybody else in the world is a sinner, too. Even Mrs. Beckwith, my tenderhearted kindergarten teacher who let me bring Pokey, my pet turtle, to class every other Monday.

The bad thing about being a sinner is that it guarantees a one-way ticket to hell. It was a little hard getting a handle on hell, beings I hadn't traveled much further than the Kansas border. But, according to my dad, hell was not a place you want to be. It was hotter than my Aunt Gwen and Uncle Ted's house in Texas the summer their air-conditioner broke. And, unlike that vacation that ended after four days, you stay in hell for eternity. To understand eternity, he said, you think of how you felt last December 26th waiting for Christmas again.

The escape clause is that you can "get saved."

So when I was four-years-old, with the church organist playing "Just As I Am," I walked to the front of the little Methodist church in Canton, Kansas, plopped down on my knobby little four-year-old knees, and asked the good lord to "forgive me for my sins." My family, a long line of Methodists, collectively breathed a sigh of relief. Dad and Mom called all the aunts and uncles that very night to broadcast the good news.

"Well, our oldest is officially saved now," they crowed proudly. "At least, we can be assured that Pam is going to heaven."

The best part, they figured, is that my conversion couldn't help but set a good example for my sister, Becki, who was two, and my brother Bobby, who was only three-months-old, although I secretly hoped they would give him until he was old enough to talk.

Course, you didn't want to take any chances. I mean, Jesus could come back at any time—night or day. He was like a thief in the night. He could come in the morning while you were stirring circles in your Captain Crunch cereal. He could come at recess while you're hanging from your knees on the monkey bars. He could even come at 2 in the morning while you were sleeping, which could be a real problem if you happen to be a heavy sleeper. Jesus could snatch you up before you had time to get the sleep out of your eyes.

And that you didn't EVEN want to think about. I mean, Aunt Gwen and Uncle Ted's house was hot.

At the same time I was learning to accept my true sinful identity, I was being told over and over again that, "God is love." Never mind that the churches presented God as a sort of hidden camera that watched over everything I did.

It made no rational sense. But what did I know? I was only four.

Even though I was yawningly close to being a perfect kid (I made straight "A's," tried not to fight with my siblings, stayed away from drugs and alcohol, and even made my bed without being told), I felt I was constantly being critiqued by this "loving God" who was sitting up in heaven, gleefully rubbing his hands together whenever I screwed up. Which, gosh darn it, (oops, there I go again, using his name in vain) seemed to be pretty often.

GOD AS TERRORIST

> "I don't know if God exists, but it would certainly be better for his reputation if he didn't."
> —Jules Renard

Phineas Parkhurst Quimby used to say that if even half of what we believed about God were true, he would be the worst of all tyrants.

No offense to Pat Robertson, but the churches and religions of the world have done a huge disservice to Cosmo K. They've taken this really cool force, this transcendant power, and turned it into a dreaded scared tactic. They've stripped God of all compassion, oneness, unity, peace, and mysticism. Their duck and cover theology has convinced us that we are the "bad guys" and that the only one wearing a white hat, the only one who can untie us from the railroad track is Jesus.

As I said, we are badly misinformed.

WHAT'S UP IS DOWN, WHAT'S IN IS OUT, WHAT'S TRUE IS FALSE

> "The god of the cannibals will be a cannibal, of the crusaders a crusader, of the merchants a merchant."
> —Ralph Waldo Emerson

Ask the average individual if he believes in God and he will probably say, "Well, duh!" However, it's unlikely he will have ever asked himself exactly what he means by God. When pressed, he'd probably answer with some cliché about "the guy upstairs."

Like these clichés, the God we've come to believe in is purely an invention of man. We made him up. Or rather the churches made him up to keep us in line. They fabricated God for the sake of convenience, based their teachings on human experience, not on deep, spiritual truth.

By now this God behaving badly is so firmly established in our consciousness that it never even occurs to us to question it. It's an opinion planted thousands of years ago that has since grown into a jungle so thick that it never dawns on us to hack our way out.

We accept this God made by man as an indisputable fact. After all, it has been substantiated by ages and ages of Bible interpretation, hasn't it?

But it makes no sense. If God is love, if God is perfect, if God is good, why would he toss anyone into a lion's den? Furthermore, why would anyone in their right mind want to hook up with a capricious and unjust god who gets his jollies from punishing them? Even the ditziest of women knows theoretically that she shouldn't hang out with a guy who might hurt her.

I mean, who needs it?

THE TEN PREVAILING FABRICATIONS ABOUT GOD:

"Our ideas of God tell us more about ourselves than about Him."
– Thomas Merton

MYTH #1: GOD IS A HIM.

Even though the progressive churches sometimes refer to God as "she," the God force doesn't really have a gender. We certainly don't talk about Mrs. Electricity or Mr. Gravity. The more appropriate pronoun for God would be "It." God is a force field that runs the universe, a powerful energy source that constantly pushes for wholeness, for growth, for change. It's the same power that grows flowers, that scabs over skinned knees. Not only is God not a him, it's not a person at all.

God is more like the force in *Star Wars*, a presence that dwells within us, a principle by which we live. All of us use "the force" all the time. Our thoughts, our bodies, our consciousness are all vibrating waves of energy. Instinctively, we all know this. That's why Luke Skywalker and Darth Vader have become such a phenomenon. *Star Wars* is a myth that speaks to us at a deep, gut level. Some part of us knows that "the force is with us" and that we, through our words, thoughts and deeds, create the world. In fact, it is not too much to say that if you catch the true concept of God, you will be swept up in a new consciousness that can revolutionize your life.

MYTH #2: GOD LOOKS LIKE ZZ TOP, MAKES BLACK CHECKMARKS AFTER YOUR NAME, AND IS BASICALLY TOO BUSY WORKING ON WORLD HUNGER TO CARE ABOUT YOU.

God, if you believe the preachers, is a little like Boo Radley, this mysterious neighbor constantly peering out the window of his penthouse suite, waiting to catch us doing something "naughty, naughty." We can't really see him, but we've been properly warned that he's there. Watching. Judging. Monitoring our every move. If you don't follow this commandment or if you break that commandment, God just might send his angel secret service after you to bop you on the head like little bunny foo-foo.

Nobody would ever admit to thinking of God as a person, but we all do. We can't help it. It's our nature to lump things together, to try to make sense of things. The reptilian part of our brains likes order, likes to understand things—even if it is limited and wrong. Whenever something trips us up, we find a box that we do understand to squeeze it into.

Like parents. We tend to think of God as a father, a guy who keeps us in line, a guy who might love us, but has to (this-is-going-to-hurt me-worse-than-it-hurts-you) punish us.

While we wouldn't go so far as to send cards on Father's Day, we openly call God "our father" and in so doing assign him with characteristics we find in our human fathers. Some of these attributes are good. Some of them are bad. All of them are wrong.

By clothing God in human form we might get someone to talk to, but we also end up with a divine busybody who changes his mind, holds grudges, and takes revenge. This inaccurate image of God forever stands in our way.

When we use expressions like "God's will, "the hand of God," "God watches over you," even "God loves you" we're only reinforcing the idea that God has human qualities. Only a fool would trust a god that's anything like him.

MYTH #3: GOD PLAYS FAVORITES.

Once again, the churches have led us to believe we need an intermediary, that we have to go through them to get to God. That's completely false. God is a force field and is equally available to everyone.

We've also been taught that some people have spiritual power and others don't. We've been taught that Jesus and Buddha and other spiritual geniuses have a special power. Sorry, Charlie. You lost out. The truth is that God, which is love, peace, and everything good, is a natural capacity in all of us, not an exclusive gift to a few.

We all have God within us. In fact, that is the primary lesson Jesus taught. God is within. You are part of God. You can perform miracles. Unfortunately, church bigwigs didn't like that idea—how in the heck were they going to control people and collect tithes if the people were out there performing their own miracles?—so they did what any good thinking dictator would do. They rewrote Jesus' teachings.

In fact, to worship Jesus the way we do is a little like worshipping Benjamin Franklin because he first discovered electricity. Ben Franklin sent that kite up in an electric storm so we could use the principle he demonstrated. He didn't do it so we'd build temples to him, paint pictures of him, and wear little keys around our necks. He wanted us to take the principle of electricity and use it . . . which we do to run radios and computers and air-conditioners. Had we stopped with Ben's discovery the way we did with Jesus' discovery, we'd all be sitting in the dark.

Benjamin Franklin didn't invent electricity anymore than Jesus invented spiritual principles. Lightning and the resulting electricity have always been available. We just didn't realize it or know how to access it. Galileo didn't invent gravity when he dropped the wooden ball off the leaning tower of Pisa. He just demonstrated it.

Likewise, Jesus demonstrated spiritual principles that he wants us to use and develop. We've wasted 2000 years worshipping this idol of him instead of using the principles he taught us. Look through the Bible and nowhere does Jesus say, "worship me." His call to us was "follow me." There's a big difference.

By making Jesus out to be a hero, we miss the whole point. Jesus wasn't saying, "I'm cool. Make statues of me, turn my birthday into a huge commercial holiday." He was saying, "Here, look what is possible. Look what we humans are capable of."

Jesus is our brother, our legacy, the guy we're supposed to emulate.

What Jesus was trying to tell us is that the churches, the religious leaders, and all their blaring rhetoric has drowned out God's truth. They've pulled the wool over our eyes by failing to mention the fact that God is not just an object of worship, but a very real presence and a principle by which we should live.

MYTH #4: GOD IS JUST SO DEMANDING.

The Ten Commandments are just the beginning. If you believe the churches, there are rules for everything—how much of your salary to stick in the offering plate, how much of your day to spend in prayer, how to treat your mother, your father, your pet Chihuahua. But here's the truth: God needs nothing. God requires nothing of us to be happy. God is happiness itself. Therefore, God requires nothing of anyone or anything in the universe. God knows nothing of sin, nothing of want, nothing of lack of any kind.

Despite what those Bible-beating TV evangelists have told you, God takes nothing personally. The God force is pure love, tolerance, compassion, generosity, beauty, gentleness, joy and, get this, completely uninterested in that extra beer you drank last night or that time you called your brother, "Mr. Poopy Pants." As far as the God force is concerned, you walk on water. There's no ring-around-the-collar, bad breath, or any adjective whatsoever that falls anyplace in a thesaurus except under love.

The God force doesn't judge. It doesn't punish. It doesn't think, "Well, Sammy C. was a good boy yesterday, helping that little old lady across the street. I think I'll answer his prayer about winning the lottery."

Those are thoughts Sandra Day O'Connor might think. Or Freddy Krueger. God doesn't make judgments or play favorites. It doesn't like Mother Teresa more than Celine Dion.

Only misinformed humans, scrambling desperately to make sense of their world, came up with a God who plays *eenie-minie-mo* with our lives, a God who likes and dislikes the same people we do. It's because we're angry and judgmental that we project those characteristics onto God.

There's no getting around it. We are violent people—emotionally if not physically. We've been brought up in a world that doesn't put love first and where love is absent fear sets in. And our fear has trapped us into a box that plays out our very limited perception. So whether we admit it or not, we have a tendency to see God as a person, as someone like us. We have made him up to fit our feeble, puny, whiny understanding.

This is going to come as a big shock to an awful lot of people, but there is also no such thing as right and wrong. There is only what works and what doesn't work, depending upon what it is that you seek to be, do, or have.

MYTH #5: GOD REWARDS OUR SUFFERING, GIVES BROWNIE POINTS FOR OUR SACRIFICE BETTER KNOWN AS "LIFE SUCKS AND THEN YOU DIE."

Most of us think life is some sort of boot camp for heaven. We believe this short life span is "only a test" for the paradise we're eventually going to earn. If we hang on and bear up, we'll someday walk through those pearly gates and be happy. These errors in thinking have been condensed into living facts. Nothing is plainer than the inevitability of sorrows and trials.

But what if it isn't necessary? What if there is no reason to be poor? Or sick? Or do anything but live an abundant, exciting life? What if these tragic, difficult lives are another rumor made up by the churches and cemented into our consciousness by years and years of conditioning?

What I'd like to suggest is this heaven you're waiting for is available now. And that you've been sold a bill of goods about who you are and what is possible.

This "sacrifice" you're unselfishly giving is a notion totally foreign to God. In fact, sacrifice and God energy are polar opposites. The God force is about growth, wholeness, and joyful living. God would never, ever, ever have anything but your very best interests at heart. And you've been given a snow job by anybody who tells you that being sick is God's will, that being poor is God's will. God's will is whatever your will is. In fact, your mind contains the God energy and therefore what you think and focus on comes into being.

You're probably thinking, "Yeah, right! Easy for you to say." But what I'm saying and what this book is all about—is don't take my word for it. Test it out. Give it a try.

The way I figure it there are only four reasons we aren't all joyous, loving freedom fighters:

1. We didn't know we could be.

2. We didn't ask.

3. We don't use our mind power properly. I don't know if you've ever been in a sailboat, but if you have, you know that unless you hold the sails in the right position, you're pretty much stuck paddling in circles. The wind, like your mind, is a potent energy source, but it won't take you anywhere until you learn the proper way to use it.

4. We like drama. Ever wonder why roller coasters are so popular? Why movies like *Alien v. Predator* boost ticket sales? C'mon, admit it, you crane your neck around to see those mangled bodies lying there along the side of the road after a car accident. You actually like being a little off-kilter and guess what? As long as you enjoy this, you get to have it.

MYTH #6: YOU DON'T WANT TO ASK TOO MUCH FROM GOD, AND CERTAINLY WOULDN'T WANT TO BUG HIM.

As I've already pointed out, God is not a person so therefore you cannot bug him.

God is a power, an unseen spiritual force. It isn't finite or limited so you certainly couldn't ask too much of it. As the old saying goes, you can take an eyedropper or a bucket to the ocean. The ocean doesn't care. If anything we don't use the God power nearly enough. This is an all-powerful force we're talking about here, not some last-minute relief team that comes in to pay the mortgage. God is not an adversary that has to be coaxed to the bargaining table.

The God force simply follows the energy you send out. Our thought vibrations draw similar vibrations. Here's an example: I once thought to myself that I'd like a potato masher. I didn't mention it to anyone. I just made a mental note, "Next time you're at Wal-Mart, buy a potato masher." That very night, my friend Wendy, who was cleaning out her drawers, stopped by with a couple no-longer-needed cooking tools including a potato masher. Another time, I decided I needed more laughter in my life. Within a couple weeks, I met and began dating Todd, a funny co-worker who eventually became a comedian.

The coincidences we see in our lives are just "the force" at work. Most of the time, we employ the force inadvertently, totally oblivious to the fact that what we think, say, and do makes a difference. Consequently, we constantly activate this power to follow the patterns we already believe in.

MYTH #7: GOD DOESN'T ANSWER. I MUST NOT HAVE FAITH.

Oh, you have faith, my friend. But you have faith in the wrong things.

Over the years, the gods have always been used as scapegoats for things we don't understand. Look at Greek mythology. If something doesn't compute in our limited brains, we say, "See, the Gods are really pissed off. They're taking it out on us." We'll grab at any explanation to avoid taking responsibility ourselves. We're like six-year-olds looking for someone to blame, always pointing fingers outside ourselves. So what if I ate sugar and red meat all my life, didn't exercise much. This cancer must be God's will.

MYTH #8: GOD IS JUST SO VAGUE.

Au contraire. Once you get rid of the black cloud of rumors and half-truths that hide your awareness of God, you'll find the unseen force communicates just as clearly as Dr. Laura. Once you rid yourself of the blocks, you'll be shown exactly what to do and how to do it. Like Maxwell Smart, you'll be given specific assignments complete with individualized instructions on how to proceed.

Again, the churches have gotten a lot of mileage out of steeping God in mystery and superstition. Since he's so obtuse, they tell us, we'd better listen to them.

Again, we need to condition ourselves to think of God more like we think of electricity. Electricity doesn't care who plugs in a curling iron. Electricity doesn't ask us to prove we're good enough to make toast.

MYTH #9: GOD ONLY ANSWERS WHEN HE'S GOOD AND READY.

There is never a time when God or "the force" isn't guiding you. And you do not have to wait for any green lights or "Get out of jail free" cards. The big guy is available 24/7 once you're ready to focus your full attention on him.

MYTH #10: GOD CREATED THE HEAVENS AND THE EARTH.

Admittedly, this is one of the toughest myths to debunk. If God didn't make this mess, who in the heck did? This may be a hard pill to swallow, but we—you and me—made the mess we call material reality. If you look very closely at what we politely assume to be the building blocks of the universe, you'll discover they're dicey at best. Or to put it another way, as renowned physicist Briane Greene did in the *New York Times,* "Quantum fluctuations so mangle space and time that the conventional ideas of left/right, backward/forward, up/down, and before/after become meaningless." In other words, we're experiencing war and global warming because that's what we've come to expect, what we look for, what we think is reality. We created these disasters with our angry, fearful consciousness. The exciting thing about this truth (that it's us, not God) is that another way IS possible. We do not have to accept war and sickness and injustice. We, by changing our consciousness, can create a peaceful world that works for everyone. It *is* possible. And this is what we must continue to look for.

We have a huge tendency to dub things we don't understand, "God's will." But God can't be blamed if there's not peace in your relationships. If your body has cancer. Those things aren't God's will. God's will, let me repeat, is one thing and one thing only—love, love, love.

And while we're on the topic of God's will, let's get this out on the table. There is no place in our updated picture of God for a hell of everlasting torment or for a misogynist that would or could attempt to put you there. Nor is there any room for the idea that sickness or deformity or death or poverty or limitation of any kind is the will of God. The will of God, if you insist on using that term, is the ceaseless longing of the spirit in you to become all you're capable of being. Amen.

PLENTY OF CHRISTIANS, NOT ENOUGH LIONS: A WHOLE NEW PARADIGM

"You can never change things by fighting the existing reality. To change something, build a new model that makes the existing model obsolete."
—Buckminster Fuller

The fact that the crucifix and Jesus' intense suffering is the central theme of Christianity should have been a dead give-away that something is all screwed up. Like the little boy who hollered, "The king has no clothes on," somebody should have stood up a long time ago and screamed at the top of their lungs "The Christian church has severely distorted the big cheese's message."

So how did this happen? Remember that game "telephone" we played as kids? One person whispers something in somebody's ear. And then that person repeats it into the ear of the next person. By the time it gets to the end of the circle, a simple statement such as the "The sky is blue" ends up being something like "Abraham Lincoln wears army boots."

I mean keep in mind that the printing press wasn't even invented until 1450 years after Jesus whispered his profound truths into the ears of his disciples. How could his message NOT have gotten a little misconstrued?

Am I suggesting we all take up the stance of Nietzsche's madman who lit a candle and ran through the marketplace, declaring, "God is dead?" that we put God out of his misery rather than allow him to hang out like some doddering, unwanted, old fool? No, that would be throwing the baby out with the bathwater. Nietzsche was right on in suggesting that the Christian conception of God was corrupt, but instead of planning a funeral, maybe we should simply drive a stake through the heart of our old beliefs.

Albert Einstein once said that the most important decision any of us ever make is whether the universe is friendly or not. This book will also ask you to make the following decisions:

Is there a benevolent force or not?

Are we guided or not?

Is the world sufficient or not?

Are your fellows for you or against you?

Is the world material or spiritual?

So which is it, fear or love?

Last summer, I learned about paradigm shifting from Lance Polingyouma, a thirty-something Hopi Indian whose father is the official storyteller of the Hopi nation.

Lance, who was trained back East as an anthropologist and archeologist, has a fascinating understanding of his culture and you might assume that he used some great Hopi legend about cacti or kachinas to change my paradigm. Oh, how wrong you'd be.

Instead, Lance asked me one simple, pointed question. "Do you ever eat Starburst?"

"Of course," I replied. "How can you grow up in America without getting at least a few packages at Halloween?"

"How do you eat them?" he continued.

"Well, I peel the wrapper off each candy, toss it in my mouth, and enjoy the lime, the orange, the lemon, or the cherry flavor."

"Have you ever tried a lime and an orange starburst together?" he asked. "At the same time. In the same mouth."

Why I'd never thought of that before. Had I not met Lance, I might still be eating Starburst one at a time, missing out on all that juicy fun.

CHAPTER 2:

LINING UP YOUR DUCKS . . . OR WHAT PRAYER IS

> "Great spirit is everywhere. It is not necessary to speak to him in a loud voice. He hears whatever is in our minds and hearts."
>
> —Black Elk

Prayer, as far as most of us are concerned, is a desperate S.O.S. reserved for special occasions. We think we're "praying" only when addressing God directly with some screech for "HELP!" But since Cosmo K is the force field that runs the universe, every thought we have is a prayer.

Every time we think any thought—be it a silent "God, doesn't she realize that skirt makes her look like Walter Matthau" to "I'll commit hari-kari if I don't get that raise"—we influence the force field. I think I should probably repeat this: every single thought affects the force field.

The only reason we don't change water into wine or heal cancer with one touch is because our thoughts (our prayers) are scattered all over the place. Instead of being one, constant, well-aimed tuning fork, our thoughts are more like a junior high band of beginning trumpet players.

On one hand, we "pray" for things to work out, but on the other, we worry they won't. At the same time we speak for good, we secretly smirk that optimism is a bunch of baloney. We want to be committed to so and so, but what if he leaves? We want to make money, but didn't the Bible say something about rich people, camels, and eyes of a needle?

The force is literally bouncing off walls. Go this way. No wait. Go that way. The force is knocking around like a lightning bug in a Mason jar. It's being dissipated because we have no clear bead on what we really want. It's not that God or "the force" isn't answering our prayers. It's just that we're "praying" for too many things.

When you figure the average person has something like 60,000 thoughts a day, you come to realize that your life experience is "prayed" about by a heck of a lot more than the "please, God, let me get out of this speeding ticket" you uttered when you first noticed the flashing red light.

Sure, you begged God for peace of mind today, but you also spent 1200 thoughts obsessing about that damned co-worker who stole your website idea. Yes, you pleaded the money case with God, but you also spent 500 thoughts worrying about your overdue car payment. When you understand prayer for what it really is, it's easier to understand why that one-time plea to the big guy doesn't always pan out.

The only reason Jesus could walk on water was because 100 percent of his thoughts (prayers) believed he could. He had overcome the world's thought system that says, "Only an idiot would be stupid enough to step out of the boat." There was not one doubt, not a single thought (prayer) in his consciousness that didn't fully believe it.

Your mind is very powerful, no matter how badly you disrespect the privilege, no matter how ineffectual you feel. Every single thought produces form at some level. Just because those thoughts are screwed up (and believe me, if you're a human, some of your thoughts are screwed up) doesn't make them weak or ineffective. Weak and ineffective at getting what you want, maybe, but never weak and ineffective.

PRAY? WHO ME?

"Prayer is a soul's sincere desire, uttered or unexpressed."
—Old hymn

People often tell me, "I don't pray. It's a waste of time. It's like believing in Santa Claus or the tooth fairy." My response? It's impossible to stop praying. Can't be done. Thomas Merton, the Christian mystic, said, "We pray by breathing."

Take Al Unser, for example. He didn't call it praying, but when he won his fourth Indianapolis 500, five days before his 48th birthday, he demonstrated the true power of prayer.

That year, 1987 to be exact, he had been unceremoniously dumped from his race team even though he'd won the Indy 500 three times before. For the first time in 22 years, it looked as if he'd be forced to watch the famous race from the sidelines. His sponsors and pretty much everyone else wrote him off as "all washed up."

But in his mind, in every thought he possessed, he knew he was not too old to race. He knew he could still win. That "prayer" was so strong that when Danny Ongais, one of the drivers who had replaced him on the team, banged himself up in practice, Unser was brought in to race a backup car, a used March-Cosworth.

Nobody except him expected anything. Not only was he driving an older model used car, but when the familiar "Gentlemen, start your engines!" rang through the P.A. system, Unser was stuck back in the 20th position.

But that didn't phase the three-time winner. In every fiber of his body, he saw himself winning. He expected nothing but victory. Finally, on the 183rd lap, he worked his way up the field, crossing the line for his fourth Indianapolis 500 title. Al Unser never had a doubt. Every single thought "prayed" for victory.

Or think of the mother, who having never before picked up anything heavier than a grocery bag of frozen foods, suddenly lifts a three-ton Plymouth off her first grade son. At that moment, she is so thoroughly engrossed in her urgent need to move that car off her precious child that she has no room for other thoughts. "I've got to move that car" was the only "prayer" in her mind. She did not remember, anywhere in her mind, that such an act was impossible.

NEWTON'S FIRST LAW OF PRAYER

"I'm 32 flavors and then some."
—Ani DiFranco

When you throw a tennis ball in the air, you can count on it coming down. Granted it might fall in the neighbor's petunias or on the roof of the 7-11 where you'll need a ladder to retrieve it, but it's guaranteed to come back down.

Prayer (thought) is just like that tennis ball. It comes back just the way you send it out. Like Newton said in his famous 4th law of energy, for every action there is an equal and opposite reaction. What you give out, what you "pray" about, you get back in equal measure. If you send out fear thoughts, you get things to be scared of. If you lie, you'll be lied to. If you criticize, you get criticized. But on the other hand, if you send out love, you get big, boun-teous love. If you send out blessings, you get blessed in equal measure.

Everything you "pray" about eventually externalizes. Or to put it another way, your inner thoughts are continually being cut and pasted into your outer life. If you want to know what you're really "praying" for, take a look around your life. You'll see your innermost thoughts, the real desires of your heart, the prayers no one knows about but you.

I knew a girl who was paranoid of spiders. She used to worry that she'd reach into her makeup drawer some morning and instead of grabbing a lipstick, put her mitts around a big, fat spider. This unfounded thought passed through her brain every morning for months until . . . guess what? She reached into her makeup drawer and grabbed a big fat, hairy wolf spider.

To put it another way, thought is creative. The thoughts you hold in your mind, both conscious and unconscious, create what you see in your life. Every thought (prayer) has a certain vibration. It boomerangs back to you according to its pitch, intensity, and depth of feeling. Your thoughts show up in your life in equal measure as their constancy, intensity, and power.

SHOOT-OUT AT THE OK CORRAL OR HOW YOUR MIND WORKS

"You always said to be true to ourselves. Which self are
we supposed to be true to?"
—Buddy (AKA Syndrome) in *The Incredibles*

Your mind is engaged in an ongoing showdown between different, conflicting parts of yourself. These splintered intentions or prayers, if you will, set all sorts of dynamics into motion. Let's say you have a conscious intention to buy a new house and you pray to find one. At the same time you set that intention into motion, you simultaneously send out an unconscious, but equally effective, fear of a higher mortgage payment. You start fretting about interest rates, start worrying about the termite contract you inadvertently let expire on your current house, both of which send out even more unconscious intentions. If these unconscious fear intentions are stronger than the conscious desire intentions, well, guess which one wins?

The dynamic of opposing "prayers" (and again, every thought is a prayer) can produce confusion and doubt. As you become open to new perceptions and desires and simultaneously experience fear and anguish, you set up a struggle.

If it keeps up, you start to doubt that prayer even works. Or at least you conclude it doesn't work for you. You become discouraged and start believing that life and circumstances are more powerful than you are.

Believe me, they're not. Not even close. Your conflicting "prayers" are simply creating turbulence in the flow of God's light.

Let me just repeat—prayer is extremely powerful. But it doesn't respond only to your pleas. It responds to every intention—conscious and unconscious—with opposing sides battling it out. Here are four of the most common battlefields:

1. THE RUT.

We humans have this annoying tendency to fall into habit patterns. Remember those 60,000 daily thoughts I mentioned earlier? Well, 59,412 of those thoughts are the exact same thoughts you had yesterday. Scientists tell us 98 percent of our thoughts are repeats from the day before.

I once had a neighbor with an invisible dog fence. You couldn't see it, but if her little jack terrier even dared step foot outside that fence, he got a painful shock. All of us are like that little jack terrier—stuck in our invisible fences.

Instead of using our prayers to think up new ideas, to ask for meaning to life's great mysteries, we waste them on trivial, insignificant, thoroughly meaningless things. Look at the cover of a typical women's magazine:

Lose inches fast

Last-minute strategies for holiday glam

Quiz: *Does your mate really love you?*

Don't we have anything better to think about?

If the 7 million readers of *Ladies Home Journal* would all wonder instead, "What can I do to improve my own soul?" or "How could I make the world more loving?" the big problems we're so afraid of would be solved in a year. Seven million people concentrating on issues like that are an unstoppable force.

2. THE AD MAN'S COPY.

U.S. advertisers spend more than $250 billion every year trying to convince you that without their products, you are a complete and total loser. The ad shill's entire reason for being is to make you and me dissatisfied with what we have and who we are. The average American sees between 1500 and 3000 commercials per day. Even non-TV watchers are constantly being invited to consume. Everything from ATM monitors to dry cleaning bags to stickers on supermarket fruit has been known to beer ads.

The most dangerous ads, as far as I'm concerned, are the new drug ads. Madison Avenue has already done a stellar job training us to need deodorant, mouthwash, and Domino's three medium-one topping pizzas for $5 each. Now, they're breaking new ground by telling us we *need* a certain medicine, and thereby training us to be sick.

3. OTHER PEOPLE'S HEADS.

Like radio waves that fly around in the atmosphere, other people's thoughts constantly bombard you. You unconsciously pick up the thoughts of your family, your culture, and your religion, even if you don't go to church. I read an article about a guy who had invented dozens of products including many that you and I use on a daily basis. He was regularly dubbed, "a genius." But if you gave him George Bush's "No Child Left Behind" test, he'd have been sent back to first grade. The guy never learned to read. And he said that was intentional.

"If I had learned to read," he said, "I'd pick up other people's ideas and cement those in my head. I choose not to bother with the interference."

In fact, the reason most of the spiritual big cheese meditate is because it helps them avoid the interference. It helps them tap into the Universal thought that is goodness, beauty, and light.

4. YOUR OWN HEAD.

Despite what you may think you're praying for, it's quite likely there's an even bigger prayer getting in the way. Unfortunately, all of us have an underlying prayer that goes something like this:

"There's something wrong with me."

"I'm not good enough."

"I have no talent."

"I don't deserve it."

"It's too hard."

Sweeping negative statements like these are what we call false prayers, the default beliefs to which you march in obedience. The good news is they're not true. The bad news is they operate as if they were true. They're your own personal amulet that you carry unwittingly everywhere you go. You wouldn't dream of plowing through life without them because, well, they're just so . . . familiar. But the problem is these particular rabbit's feet are concrete and weigh 189 pounds. They sap your strength, shackle your potential, and knock your hopes to hell and gone.

When I first began writing for magazines, I had an inferiority complex that wouldn't have fit in Shea Stadium. Because I was from a small town in the Midwest, I couldn't imagine that I had anything to say to a fancy editor from New York. Although I sent query after query pitching my many ideas, I didn't really expect to sell too many. After all, I just "knew" there "weren't enough" assignments to go around. At best, I figured I might be able to sneak a few under the cracks.

Needless to say, I got a lot of rejection letters, so many that I probably could have wallpapered the city of Cincinnati should they have needed wallpaper. The editors didn't exactly tell me to drop dead, but they didn't encourage me to keep writing either.

Then I read a book called *Write for your Life* by Lawrence Block. In the early eighties, when his column for *Writer's Digest* was at the height of its popularity, he and his wife, Lynn, decided to throw a series of seminars for writer-wannabes.

They called the day-long seminars "Write for your Life" and set about booking hotel rooms in cities around the country. Unlike most writing seminars where you learn to write plot treatments or how to get an agent, Block's seminar dealt with the only thing that really matters when it comes to being a writer: Getting out of your own way. Getting rid of the countless negative thoughts that tell you what a hopelessly uninteresting specimen of humanity you are.

At the seminar, participants meditated, grabbed partners and confessed their greatest fears and did all kinds of things that helped them get to the bottom of why they wanted to write, but didn't.

The seminars were hugely successful, but Block, who was a writer, not a seminar-giver, eventually got tired of trotting around the country, collecting tickets. Instead, he self-published the book that I ran into about the same time.

I took the book to heart. I did all of the exercises. I wrote affirmations. I consulted my inner child to find out what I was so afraid of. I even sent myself postcards for 30 days straight. On these postcards, I'd write such affirming reminders as "You, Pam, are a great writer." "You, Pam, have what it takes to sell to New York editors." "You, Pam, are interesting and people want to hear what you have to say."

I'm sure the postman thought I was a little cracked, wasting 25 cents or whatever the postage was back then to send myself a postcard telling myself I was fascinating and abundant. But if he knew what a change it made in my life, he'd have been doing it, too.

Suddenly, I started getting assignments from the big national magazines with, yes, the big New York editors. First, there was *Modern Bride* that wanted a piece on exercises couples could do together. *Ladies' Home Journal* asked for a travel story on Tampa Bay. Suddenly, this once-insecure writer from Kansas was getting assignments from big national magazines, the kind of magazines you see in dentists' offices.

Did I suddenly start writing more fluidly, coming up with more compelling ideas? Probably a little bit (after all, that was one of my affirmations), but mostly I changed the reality of what I thought and said about myself.

I gave up the "prayer" that there "weren't enough" assignments to go around. I let go of the "prayer" that I wasn't talented enough to sell to national magazines.

If you're not getting answers to what you formerly thought of as prayer, you have to take into consideration the other thoughts you formerly "prayed." To bring about "God's truth in form" you have to get all those ducks flying in the same direction. Once they're all quacking for the same thing, you'll get nothing but health, wealth, love, friends, and perfect self-expression.

GETTING THE DUCKS TO QUACK IN UNISON.

"The main thing is to keep the main thing the main thing."
—T-shirt I saw in Hawaii

Filmmaker Michael Moore, in a 2002 commencement speech, gave the following advice. "All you boys should learn that once you give up on that girl, she will come to you."

In some ways, prayer works the same way. By believing we desperately need prayer or a miracle or something we don't have now, we deny God's truth. We suit up with the wrong attitude.

Any time we look for an answer, we make the false assumption that the answer isn't already here. Praying for love or happiness or some other desired goal defeats the whole purpose. It assumes somehow that the outcome of life is still in doubt. It's not. God's truth is perfection, all-joy, all-love, and to crave some piddling commodity is believing there's something else. You have to suit up with perfect confidence that you have the right for all that is good. In fact, you have to believe it's already here.

To Jesus, prayer was not a matter of bribing God. It was simply understanding that the higher law of Spirit overrides the lower law of the mental and physical plane. To plead or beg or to act like it's not here is to suppose duality, not unity. And unity is what we're going for. To get those ducks lined up, to get all those waves in laser-like coherence.

LIKE A LASER, TOUCHED FOR THE VERY FIRST TIME

"We can't afford the luxury of doubt."
—Elastigirl in *The Incredibles*

I don't know if you know anything about laser technology, but it works a little bit like Congress did on September 12, 2001. Remember how all those cantankerous old senators and representatives completely forgot they were Republicans and Democrats, liberals and conservatives? How the only thing in their minds were "I'm an American, by God" and they sang "God Bless America" in one great, big unified chorus? Well, that's how a laser works.

Unlike ordinary light, that has lots of different types and sizes of wavelengths, lasers have one size wavelength, each of which precisely reinforces every other.

This is how you want to pray. Or it is if you want to see something appreciable happen. When Jesus "prayed" to multiply the fish and loaves, he didn't beg God to "make something happen," he simply put all his thoughts into one laser-like formation, namely that abundance and plenty was his divine right.

In fact, the real reason Jesus was crucified was because those in command thought he was altogether too confident. How dare he be so bold as to think he could make crippled people walk, lepers dance? But Jesus didn't just think he could do these things. He knew. He knew the truth of who he was which made his mind a veritable laser. He didn't doubt for one second there was plenty of food to go around. He didn't stop to question if a blind man could see (after all, the gift of health and perfect self-expression is everyone's divine right) or if that storm that so scared the disciples was real. He knew that he had the right to command the heavens and the earth. In fact, that's the only real difference between Jesus and you and me. We're still wondering.

If you go back to Aramaic, which as you probably know is the language Jesus conversed in, the root word of *ask* reveals more than a "Well, if it's not too much trouble." Ask, in Aramaic, means a combination of claim (as in that deed to the land is yours) or demand. To ask for something in prayer is to simply lay hold of what's yours. You have the right, and even the responsibility to command your life.

How can we be sure, you ask? Same way you're sure two plus two equals four: Because it's a simple, unalterable principle of mathematics. If you add two plus two and get five, that's not the principle of mathematics' fault. Likewise, if you're not getting the answers you want from your prayers, that's not God's fault. It's *you* that's screwing up the principle.

With God, there is no variation. There is one perfect picture of health, abundance, joy, peace, love, and all that other good stuff. But because we, like ordinary light with its variety of wavelengths, have all these variety of thoughts, we create a lot of turbulence. But it's not necessary.

Prayer that is focused through an integrated, whole personality is like a laser—a single, clear beam. It doesn't matter who asks or how they ask. God's answer is always "love and light and peace." That's not only God's final answer, it's the only answer.

CHAPTER 3:

SPIRITUAL PRINCIPLES UNVEILED

"We live in paradise and haven't even noticed."
—Byron Katie

One of the main tenets of the *Starship Enterprise*, as they glibly zipped around the cosmos, was don't even think about interfering with an unknown planet's evolutionary pattern. At the risk of interfering in my own planet's evolutionary pattern, I now plan to fill you in on some important spiritual truths. And unlike Spock, I'm damned sure hoping they interfere with our evolutionary pattern, which if you ask me, could use some serious sprucing up:

THE FIRST STEP IN SPIRITUAL ENLIGHTENMENT IS TO GIVE UP YOUR POWERFUL ATTACHMENT TO CONVENTIONAL REALITY.

"We are all captives of a story."
—Daniel Quinn

The New York Times kicked off 2004 with one doozy of an investigatory scoop. According to a prominent scientist at Columbia University, two of the very building blocks of everyday reality—time and space—are not what they're cracked up to be. In fact, there's rock solid evidence that most of what we think of as reality is an illusion, a put on, a con job of enormous existential significance.

It's really only a matter of time before scientists will be forced to trade in their old formulation of natural law for a radically different, more accurate view of reality. Namely, that consciousness itself creates the material world. For years, Western science has operated on the assumption that consciousness emerges from, or is dependent upon, the physical world of space, time, and matter. In other words, the world is a machine, an objective world made up of atoms.

But unfortunately this dogmatic worldview has glaring gaps and major holes. There is far too much quantum weirdness going on, way too many lab results showing that the objective world is an illusion of our thinking. For example, physicists now have irrefutable proof that an electron can be in two or more places at the same time, that time can go backwards, and that once you go to the trouble to observe a wave it freezes into a particle. In other words, material reality, is nothing like it appears.

This radical view is not exactly breaking news having been fleshed out nearly a century ago by an acknowledged genius of the twentieth century. Albert Einstein and his cronies ushered in a whole new wave of energy physics that we now call quantum mechanics or the new physics.

And every physicist on the planet knows about the freaky universe where matter pops into existence from nothing at all and where electrons can jump from one orbit to another without traveling across intervening space, but most have chosen to ignore it, to shrug their shoulders, and to employ the old junior high standby, "Whatever!"

It's not that they're in total denial. They've used the new physics to develop lasers, transistors, superconductors, and atom bombs. But they can't even begin to explain how this quantum world works. As one physicist put it, "The question is not whether the theories are crazy, but whether they're crazy enough." Or as physicist James Trefil observed, "We've encountered an area of the universe our brains just aren't wired to understand."

The continued failure of science to make any appreciable headway into this fundamental problem suggests that all approaches are on the wrong track. Believe me, I understand stubbornness, but eventually even those medieval sailors had to concede that the world was not really flat.

A few brave physicists are starting to acknowledge that their precious assumptions may be wrong. They're admitting that the fundamental tenets of material reality just don't hold up. Some are even brave enough to admit that consciousness itself creates the physical world. As Fred Alan Wolf, a physicist at the University of California, says, "It boils down to this—the universe doesn't exist without a perceiver of that universe."

All I have to say is "about time."

The Course in Miracles, a self-study program in spiritual psychology that I've been studying and teaching for 15 years, has always advocated the idea that consciousness creates the material world. It says we humans decide in advance how we're going to experience life, that we choose beforehand what we want to see.

The problem is we all look at the world with a giant chip on our shoulder. All we need to do to change the course of our crummy lives is to get over our on-going grudge against the world, to actively see and expect a different reality. As it is now, we devote all our time and attention (our consciousness, if you will) to things we do not want.

But it's nothing more than a bad habit. And like any bad habit, it can be changed with conscious and deliberate effort.

Turns out that almost all the concepts and judgments we take for granted are actually distortions that our very creative minds made up. Very early on, say sometime around birth, our mind establishes a pattern of perception and then proceeds to filter out everything else. In other words, we only "experience" things that jive with our very limited perception.

A girl from the Philippines told me that it was weeks, if not months, after she arrived in the United States before she noticed that some people here had red hair, including people she knew and dealt with on a regular basis. She said red hair was inconsistent with what she had been conditioned to see and expect. So for at least a few months, she was subjectively blind to red hair.

Scientists now know that our brain receives 400 billion bits of information each second. To give you some idea of just how much information that is, consider this: it would take nearly 600,000 average size books just to print 400 billion zeroes. Needless to say, that's a heck of a lot of reality. So what do we do? We start screening. We start narrowing down. I'll take that bit of information over there and let's see this one fits nicely with my ongoing soap opera about the opposite sex. When all is said and done, we're down to 2000 measly bits of information. Go ahead and take a bow because even that's pretty impressive. We're talking 2000 bits of information each and every second. But here's the problem. What we choose to take in is only one half of one millionth of a percent of what's possible.

Let's pretend that each dot of a pen point is one bit of information. I've been practicing and the most dots I can reasonably make in one second is five. But let's be generous and assume you're a better pen dotter than me and can make 10 dots per second. Again, we're assuming that each dot is a bit of information. To make as many dots as your brain processes in one second takes nearly three and a half minutes at your highly superior rate of 10 dots per second. But if your brain were processing all the available information (400 billion dots) it would take 821 years.

Our brains continually sift through the possibilities and pick which bits of information to "see" and believe.

Out of sheer laziness, the stuff we choose to perceive (and make no mistake it IS a choice) is stuff we already know, it's stuff we decided on way back when. We see, feel, taste, touch, and smell not the real world, but a drastically condensed version of the world, a version that our brains literally concoct. The rest zooms by without recognition. John Maunsell, a neuroscientist at the Baylor College of Medicine, says, "People imagine they're seeing what's really there, but they're not."

Once your brain decides which bits to let in, it builds bridges between various nerve cells, interlacing nerve fibers to create neural pathways. The average human has 10 billion nerve cells, each with innumerable extensions, so different highways get built in each brain. The map of neural pathways in your brain and say Johnny Depp's brain are as different as the maps of Wisconsin and Rhode Island.

Once you get the pathways set up, you quit traveling the rest of the country. Interstate 70 in my home state of Kansas makes for a perfect metaphor. Believe it or not, Kansas, the state producers of *The Wizard of Oz* portrayed in black and white, actually contains lots of geological landmarks. There's a miniature Grand Canyon in the northwest corner, for example, and a huge 50-story limestone formation called Castle Rock near Quinter. But since people traveling through Kansas rarely leave I-70, nobody has a clue these geological formations exist. They've literally bypassed all the beautiful, worthwhile stuff and come to the erroneous conclusion that Kansas is flat and boring. But it's not reality.

Like those highway planners who put I-70 where they did because it was the flattest, quickest, and easiest route, we build our neural pathways on the flattest, quickest, easiest routes. But it doesn't show us reality. It's not even close (three and a half minutes compared to 821 years) to seeing all that's there.

The roads and highways of our brains get set up pretty early. When we're born, every possibility exists. Let's take language, for example. Within every newborn is the ability to pronounce every sound in every single language. The potential is there for the "r" rolling of the Spanish language. It's there for those weird German diphthongs that resemble sounds best performed in the bathroom.

But very early on, our brains lay down neural pathways that mesh with the sounds we hear every day, eliminating other sounds from other languages.

With the possible exception of Barbara Walters, pretty much everyone that speaks English can pronounce the following phrase: *Rolling Rock really rouses Roland.* But when someone from China tries to learn English, they no longer have the neural pathways to say their "r's", so that's why fried rice become "flied lice." Just so no one thinks I'm ethnocentric, I have to add that I've tried pronouncing some of those guttural German words and my German neural pathways have been shot all to hell and back.

Perhaps the best example of how your mind creates its own virtual reality game is the everyday, garden-variety dream. When Morley Safer showed up on your doorstep last night asking all those embarrassing questions, it seemed pretty darn real. But once the alarm clock went off, Morley and that virtual reality game popped like the flimsy soap bubble it was.

Our neural pathways establish reruns of what has gone before. Like the three-year-old who insists on watching *The Little Mermaid* over and over and over again, we cling to our warped illusions with a tenacious grip. Get your bloody hands off my illusion. Even though it makes us miserable, we prefer to place our faith in the disaster we have made.

THE MAGIC WE THREW OVERBOARD

**"Most people come to know only one corner of their room,
one narrow strip on which they keep walking back and forth."**
—Rainer Maria Rilke

Any illusionist worth his magic wand understands that the most important ingredient in his sleight of hand repertoire is diversion. A magician diverts his audience's attention *away* from what he's really doing and directs it *towards* something else that seems crucial, but, of course, isn't.

That's what we've done. Diverted all our attention to the physical world. The uncrucial and very irrelevant physical world. That wouldn't be a problem except that it's not really who you are. Ninety-nine percent of who you are is spiritual. These visual bluffs have caused you to miss 99 percent of who you are.

Imagine if you had a friend who put all her energy into the fingernail on her left pinky.

Let's say she paints that fingernail every day with the most beautiful of fingernail polish. She files it. She buffs it. Needless to say, she'd have a really cool left pinky fingernail. But if she totally ignores the rest of her body, suffice it to say she's probably not taking advantage of all life has to offer.

The 99 percent you're missing is the real magic. It's the magic that attracts the right people and the right opportunities. It's the force that activates the immune system, the fuel that arouses hope, creativity, infinite knowledge, and endless joy.

Your life, no matter how chaotic it may appear, contains order, peace, and harmony. All the storms whipping through your life have an unseen cause that's hidden because you've been focusing on that left pinky.

The left pinky you pay so much attention to is the realm of Murphy's Law—you know the law that states everything that can go wrong will. The left pinky is where fulfillment seems temporary and desire remains unfulfilled.

This book is about getting in touch with the other reality, a world of absolute order, perfection, spiritual light, a world where you can initiate positive, lasting change.

The perfect you isn't something you have to create. It's already there. All you need to do is quit diverting your attention to the left pinky and focus all your attention onto the truth.

PICKING ANOTHER CHANNEL

"Emancipate yourself from mental slavery. None but ourselves can free our minds."
—Bob Marley

I know you think you're being "objective." You think you're seeing "reality." But, in these experiments, be willing to consider the possibility that you're being spun by your own inaccurate and starkly limited perception. Maybe this isn't the time to mention it, but what scientists have proven is that in order to keep our stories together, we actually learn to lie to ourselves.

The purpose of this book is to release you from the imprisonment of your illusions. To do that, I'm going to ask you to suspend judgment—or at least be willing to admit that another way of looking at the world might be possible. You don't have to do it for long. All I'm asking is that for the next 21 days, the time it takes to do these experiments, you set aside the manufactured press release you believe to be reality and consider a new possibility. You don't have to change a single one of your behaviors. All you have to do is change your mind.

Is that so much to ask? A slight willingness to see things a bit differently? If you try it, find I'm blowing smoke, then, hey, feel free to resume your old thinking.

What do you have to lose? Heck, you can even get your money back on the book if you don't find convincing evidence.

IF YOU BUILD IT, THE DUDE WILL COME

"How the world still dearly loves a cage."
—Ruth Gorden in *Harold and Maude*

Okay, okay, I know you're already an "expert" at this stuff. You've read all the books. You've taken all the weekend workshops. But have you really applied yourself? Have you really put these principles into practice? On a daily, decision-by-decision basis?

I'd like to wager that, at this point, you're still a theorist, a very astute theorist no doubt, but a theorist. Theorists know spiritual principles. They don't practice spiritual principles.

But here's the deal. Understanding a theory about spirituality is akin to reading a book about yoga or watching a film about running. The difference is like the difference between George Clooney and George Clooney's phone number.

THEORISTS TEND TO KEEP SPIRITUAL PRINCIPLES AT ARM'S DISTANCE.

The other problem with theories is they occupy only a small piece of your mind. The rest of your mind, say 99.9 percent of it, is devoted to the things you think the theories will eliminate. In other words, your mind is devoted to things you do not want. It's devoted to old beliefs of scarcity, problem relationships, a God who shoots fire bolts from heaven.

Let's take being broke, for example. Most of us can agree we don't want to be broke. So what do we do? We devote our minds to avoiding it. We work long hours. We call our stockbrokers. We read books and articles about "getting rich," fully ignoring the fact that by trying to "get rich" we devote our minds to the idea that we're not already rich. Consequently, we've decided in advance to be broke.

If we simply devote our minds to feeling rich, to being grateful for all the already-apparent riches in our lives—say, our families and our wonderful friends—being broke would disappear. We only experience it because we devote our thoughts to it. That's how powerful our minds are.

The reason 99.9 percent of your mind is still devoted to things you don't want is because that's the world's default setting. That's what the world defines as normal.

The world's default setting sees news about floods and earthquakes, hears stories about your second cousin's epilepsy and says, "See what did I tell you?" It's next to impossible to override the world's default setting even though we know—at least theoretically—that another way is possible.

The purpose of this book and its ten spiritual experiments is to change your default setting. Here are the crib notes:

> **1.** There is an awesome, all-loving God force.
>
> **2.** It has a grand purpose for your life.
>
> **3.** It will continually guide you, communicate with you, give you clear instructions.
>
> **4.** It'll give you joy, peace, and contentment.
>
> **5.** It'll insure you of rich, warm, wonderful relationships.

MINDS OF STEEL

"Do not inflate plain things into marvels, but reduce marvels into plain things."
—Francis Bacon

In case you haven't checked Amazon lately, there are literally thousands of books on how to change your body. At last count, buns alone merited 317 books and tapes. But as far as I can tell, there's not a single book on how to shape your mind. Yet, your mind with all its preset, misconstrued neural pathways is the root of all your problems. Remember it is consciousness, as a few brave physicists are starting to acknowledge, that creates physical reality. Even those buns that aren't steel yet.

A friend of mine was moaning about her boyfriend's alcoholic behavior. She was disappointed because he'd gotten drunk and forgotten about a dinner party she'd invited him to or gotten drunk and spent the money they were going to use for Harry Connick Jr. tickets or gotten drunk and . . . you get the picture. I finally asked her, "Why do you persist in expecting sane behavior from an insane person?" It's like going to the shoe store to buy milk. You can go back time and time again, but that shoe store is never going to sell milk. Likewise, her boyfriend, as long as he's drinking, is never going to be sane. And all those desperate attempts to change your body, your relationship, your fill-in-the-blank are never going to work until you learn to change and shape your mind.

Your mind at this point is undisciplined, flabby, and out-of-shape. You allow it to karoom all over the place with worry, frustration, and fear that your 12-year-old daughter will become the next Courtney Love.

It's pretty difficult to control your mind when you think you have to do it forever. But by setting up a defined time frame as we do in these experiments, your mind can be coaxed into giving it a whirl. It works like the 12-step program. Trying to stay sober forever can't work. One day at a time? Now, that's something a mind can wrap itself around.

With the exception of Experiment #8, each of the experiments takes 48 hours or less. That's two short days out of a 70-year-lifespan. Even a flabby mind can commit to that.

Why do we give ourselves 48 hours? Call it the old deadline principle. When an editor gives a deadline, he or she knows to start checking for said manuscript around that time. Deadlines give us something to expect, something to look for. When you're on an unfamiliar country road looking for the green mailbox where you're supposed to turn left to your blind date's house, it helps to know it's 8.1 miles from the last turn. Otherwise, you start to wonder if you missed it and end up doubling back. Rather than putting God on the spot, a deadline simply jars you into paying attention.

Once, I asked God if I should begin freelancing full-time. I was working 20 hours a week for a small company and writing on the side.

"God," I prayed. "I really like Resource and Development (the place I was working), but I have this dream, you see, of being a full-time freelancer. It's not that I don't like writing fundraising letters, it's just that I want to pursue my own story ideas, write about the things that burn in my heart. What do you think?"

Already, I was getting lots of assignments. Big national magazines were calling. I was making new contacts, receiving nibbles on a couple column ideas. That would have been answer enough for some people.

But I'm dense. I wanted an unquestionable sign.

"God," I went on. "I need a sign that cannot be written off as coincidence. Furthermore, I'm giving you a deadline. I need to know in 24 hours."

The next day I got fired.

Another time, when my freelancing was slow, I sent out resumes, something I'm prone to do whenever I feel panicky. Sure enough, I was offered a job within a few weeks. The offer, writing marketing materials for a local bus line (okay, I didn't say I was offered an interesting job in two weeks) was for more money than I'd ever made in my life. But how could I afford to give up all that time?

Was I really ready to give up my freelancing career? I figured I'd better consult Cosmo K. Again, I prayed for a clear sign. But this time I upped the stakes. I told him he'd better speak up within 24 hours because that's when I needed to give my employer-to-be a "yea" or a "nay."

The very next morning, *Travel & Leisure*, the magazine I most wanted to write for, called to give me an assignment.

After I hung up, yelled "Yes!" and did the goal line hootchie-koo, I bowed my head and said, "Thanks." But Cosmo K must have been in the mood to show off that day because not 15 minutes later, another magazine I'd never even heard of, let alone sent a query to, called and wanted a story about Kansas City steaks. I had to call and tell my boss-to-be "Thanks, but no thanks."

The experiments in this book are bold, daring, and your friend might suspect that you've cracked. But that is the old way of thinking, the way of thinking you're now committed to changing.

To be in the kingdom, as the Course in Miracles puts it, is to merely focus your full attention on it. You have to be willing to perceive nothing else.

Unfortunately, we only see what we're looking for. Here's one small example. For years, I have frequented a little coffee shop in my hometown called La Prima Tazza. I'm not your traditional coffee drinker, but I like a mocha breve every now and again and La Prima Tazza is a great place to people-watch and talk liberal politics. A few weeks ago, a friend of mine with a more pronounced coffee habit came to Lawrence to spend a few days. She insisted that if I wanted her to be passably coherent and hospitable in the morning, I needed coffee beans (organic, free trade, shade-grown coffee beans, no less). Since I don't normally buy coffee beans, I wasn't sure where to begin. I asked the barrista, "Any ideas where to find some good coffee beans?"

Duh! La Prima Tazza has a whole shelf of beans for sale by the pound. This shelf can't be more than two-feet from the place I stood all 398 times I ordered my mocha breve. I had never noticed because it's not what I was looking for.

LIKE HOUSEBREAKING A PUPPY

"Everyone thinks of changing the world, but no
one thinks of changing himself."
—Leo Tolstoy

If your brain is anything like mine (prone to procrastination, easily confused and distractible) changing your mind can be downright challenging. I like to think of it like housebreaking a puppy.

You just keep taking it back outside and showing it a different reality until finally it realizes, "Wow, there's a whole big world out there. And it's a lot more fun to pee on trees and bushes and fire hydrants than on Pam's ratty old house slippers." Your mind will be astonished by the beauty that's available when you put it on the spot. Deep peace will appear. Great ideas will materialize and expand. Joy will rise up.

The only thing you need do is devote your mind ONLY to things you want. If you want peace, think of peace. If you want love, think of love. If you want Jimmy Choo pumps, think of Jimmy Choo pumps. Do not think about how peace looks impossible or that love seems fleeting or that there's no money in your bank account for Jimmy Choo pumps. Keep your mind focused only on what you want. And anytime that puppy starts heading towards those slippers, pick it up and take it back outside.

In the movie *Man on Fire*, Denzel Washington plays an ex-Special Forces operative who becomes a body guard to the young daughter of a wealthy Mexican businessman. Despite Denzel's attempts to stay neutral and uninvolved, he ends up becoming a father figure to

Pita, tutoring her with her homework, and helping her gain a place on the swim team, an activity she loves more than the piano lessons her father insists upon. Over and over in their swim training, Denzel shouts out the same question, "Trained or untrained?" And Pita shouts back exuberantly, "Trained!"

So I'll repeat the question. "Is your mind trained or untrained?"

And I hope you'll soon be able to shout back, "Trained."

"The greatest discovery and development of the coming years will be along spiritual lines. Here is a force which history clearly teaches has been the greatest power in the development of man and history, and yet we have been merely playing with it and have never seriously studied it as we have physical forces. Some day people will learn that material things do not bring happiness and are of little use in making men and women creative and powerful. Then the scientists of the world will turn their laboratories over to the study of God and the spiritual forces. When this day comes, the world will see more advancement in one generation than it has in the past four."

—Charles Proteus Steinmetz, inventor of the alternating current

PART TWO:

THE EXPERIMENTS

"Prove me now herewith."
—Malachi 3:10

SCIENCE BASICS

"Nothing shocks me. I'm a scientist."
—Harrison Ford, as Indiana Jones

You don't need a white lab coat, carbon nanotubes, or even those unsightly protective goggles to conduct the following do-it-yourself experiments. All you need is an open mind and the ability to observe, record your findings, and be willing to frame things in a new light.

As I mentioned, each of the following chapters presents a spiritual principle and an empirical science experiment to prove it.

Or not.

Last thing I'd ask is for you to buy into anything I know to be true or anything anybody else claims to be true. The best policy: test these spiritual principles for yourself. See if they work for you, see if they're true from YOUR experience. Feel free to be cold-blooded.

As I said, there should never be coercion in spirituality. If you take someone else's word for spiritual principles, there will always be a residue of doubt. Don't believe what anybody else says. Not one word. By conducting these experiments on your own life, in your own way, you'll find complete and certain conviction. And that's the only thing that will radically change your life.

But I guarantee that if you do any one of these experiments with the proper openness, your understanding of the world will be alchemized into a new and more useful perspective.

As I said, as long as that space heater's there, you might as well turn the danged thing on.

For those of you who flunked chemistry, we should probably start with a refresher course.

1. WHAT EXACTLY IS SCIENCE?

During the Middle Ages, there were all kinds of—how do I say this politely—utterly ridiculous theories. For example, people believed the ground-up horn of a rhinoceros could increase sexual potency and that leeches, those horrible, slimy, blood-sucking worms, sucked out disease. Even Aristotle, as smart as he might have been about philosophy, had some preposterous ideas about the way the world worked. For example, he theorized that males and females have different number of teeth. He then provided lengthy arguments as to why this theory had to be true. The only problem? He didn't bother to count.

Needless to say, that method of science is a bit unreliable. Arguments, no matter how compelling, cannot determine whether a theory is true or not. The only way to prove a theory is to conduct an experiment that can be universally reproduced by anyone. For example, the theory of gravity can be proved by anyone from a toddler jumping out of a bunkbed to a voodoo priest leaping over a sacrificial goat.

2. OKAY, SO WHAT'S A THEORY?

To most of us, a theory is a vague and fuzzy fact. But when you talk about scientific theory you're talking about a conceptual framework that explains existing observations and predicts new ones. A theory is accepted, not based on the prestige or convincing powers of its proponent, but on the results obtained through observations and/or experiments that anyone can reproduce. In other words, the results are repeatable. In fact, most lab experiments are repeated many dozens and quadrillions of times.

The other characteristic of a scientific theory is it's falsifiable meaning that an experiment could also prove that it's untrue. The theory that "Mars is populated with little green men who flee whenever we hunt them" is not falsifiable because in that theory the Martians always disappear whenever anyone tracks them. But the theory that "Martians do not exist" is scientific because you can falsify it by catching one and getting him an invitation to *Good Morning, America.*

3. THEN WHAT IS A HYPOTHESIS (HI-POTH-E-SISS)?

Again, in common vernacular a hypothesis is a synonym for "guess." But to a scientist, a hypothesis is a working assumption about how the world works. Every experiment starts with one. You make observations about how the world works and then you come up with a hypothesis that can be tested to see if it "holds water." It's usually cast as a statement that that can either be refuted or proven. It's often written as an "if-then" statement (if I do such and such, then such-and-such will happen). "If x occurs, then y will follow," or "As x increases, so will y." We use it to form a scientific method.

4. EXCUSE ME, A SCIENTIFIC METHOD?

Any scientist anywhere, whether she speaks Japanese, Farzi, or French, knows what is meant by the scientific method. It's universally accepted as being the best way for winnowing truth from lies and delusion. The simple version looks something like this:

a. State a question.

b. Form a hypothesis.

c. Test hypothesis.

d. Record and study data.

e. Draw conclusions.

The great advantage of the scientific method is that it is unprejudiced. It works the same for everyone. The conclusions will hold irrespective of your state of mind, your religious persuasion, or your shoe size.

Okay, ready to become a mad scientist?

THE DUDE ABIDES PRINCIPLE

There is a mind-boggling force that offers infinite love, tolerance, compassion, generosity, beauty, gentleness, joy, peace, and wisdom. And it's yours for the asking. Anytime, anywhere.

"I will come to you if you invite me."
—God in *Conversations with God*

This experiment will prove to you once and for all that there is a good, loving, abundant, totally hip force in the universe. You can call it God. You can call it "prana," "chi" or "the all that is." I call it Cosmo K.

The problem, up until now, is that we've had to take this "God" on faith. We weren't allowed to see him or touch him. Of course, we're asked to do lots of things for him, like tithe and meditate and put ashes on our head. Doesn't sound like much of a bargain to me. I much prefer the idea of a God who moves on a two-way street. Does give and take ring any bells?

In this experiment, we let the big guy know that, baby, it's now or never. We are sick of believing in something that gets its jollies by playing hide and seek. Going to heaven in a few years might sound like a carnival to some folks, but I want evidence now. As in right now. You know those four little initials—A.S.A.P. Well, those are the ones I'm shooting for. I am going to give you exactly 48 hours to give me a sign, a clear sign, a sign that cannot be written off. Neon would work.

We've been looking for God for centuries, but because we bought this idea he's vague and mysterious, we don't really expect to find him. Or at least we're not surprised when we don't. Because we haven't been trained to notice, this inspiring, energizing, life-altering force is zooming in, around, and through us without our awareness.

In these experiments, you're going to look for evidence of Cosmo K the same way you'd look for a set of missing car keys. On a day you're out of milk and the baby's crying.

After looking everywhere you normally put them—in your purse, in the pocket of your khakis, on the counter by the door—you start lifting up couch cushions, crawling under the bed, and sifting through kitty litter. The important thing is you don't stop looking until you're clutching them in your grubby little paws.

If you go to the grocery store for sink cleanser, you don't come home until you find the shelf with the Comet, the Ajax, and the Mr. Clean. If you go to the bookstore to pick up the latest John Grisham novel, you don't wimp out with some feeble excuse about not being able to find the "G" section.

It's not even a question of whether or not you're going to find sink cleanser or the latest John Grisham novel. You go fully-knowing they're going to be there.

At the end of each chapter, there is a lab report sheet. These are similar to the lab reports real scientists use. All you need is a pen (or a pencil or a glitter pen, for that matter) to jot down the time you launch each experiment.

This is important, because you need to be definite and crystal clear in your intention. One of the spiritual principles we'll eventually test is everybody gets out of life exactly what they're looking for. The only reason you haven't found evidence of God is because you're way too busy looking for other things.

WHAT, ME WAIT?

"If your medicine doesn't grow corn, of what use is it?"
—Sun Bear

If you want to wait until the pearly gates to find evidence of God, you go right ahead.

But that doesn't work for me. I want to use the God force now. There's this all-loving, all-giving, all-knowing, all-inspiring, all-powerful force and you want to wait and meet It at the pearly gates?

It's like a modern day person refusing to use electricity. All you have to do to access electricity is find an electrical outlet, plug in an electric appliance, and voila! You get all sorts of cool stuff—toasted bread, music that's piped in from radio towers, movies and news and fellow humanoids performing all sorts of antics like eating slugs on deserted islands.

We have to retrain ourselves to think of the God power the same way we think of electricity. We don't wonder, "Am I good enough to plug my toaster oven into the outlet?" "Have I prayed long enough or deep enough to deserve the right to flick on the kitchen lights?"

We don't feel guilty for wanting to turn on the radio and listen to NPR. The God juice is just as non-prejudiced and available as electricity once we make the decision to really look for it.

And it's not that hard to find.

You don't even need a converter when traveling in Europe. This good, loving, abundant force is everywhere available. At any time (your birthday, next Tuesday at 3 p.m., the year after), you can hook in. You just have to make the decision.

ANECDOTAL EVIDENCE:

"God is not the pushover that some people would like you to believe."
—Alex Frankovitch in *Skinny Bones*

Well, unless you just crawled out from underneath a cabbage leaf, you've probably observed that an awful lot of people talk about this guy named God. One out of every seven days is devoted to worshipping him. Buildings of all shapes and sizes have been built to honor him. Most newspapers have a religious section right next to the political section, the local news, the weather, and the crossword puzzle.

Some version of the dude exists in every culture that has ever existed. Granted, he's pretty different depending on who you talk to, but the idea of a supreme force is pretty universal. A belief in something bigger is a pull as strong as the sun.

According to *Webster's*, a physicist is a scientist who studies the properties and interactions of matter and energy. And all of them know about the invisible force. To be fair and balanced, I have to acknowledge that lots of them do not call the force God. Or even Cosmo K. Albert Einstein, for example, didn't believe in the traditional God, but he sure as heck knew there was something a whole lot juicier out there in the cosmos. In fact, that juice, he says, was all he cared about. The rest, he claimed, was just details.

THE METHOD:

"Allowing myself to become a little nutty and irrational
did open me up to certain mystical experiences."
—D. Patrick Miller

In this experiment, you're going to devote 48 hours looking for evidence of this good, all-knowing, all-perfect force. You're not required to quit your day job or schedule a special appointment. The force exists every single place you could think to look.

To up the stakes, you're going to ask the force for a blessing or what I call an unexpected gift. You're going to give The Dude 48 hours to send you a gift you wouldn't normally receive—a surprise check in the mail, a card from an old friend you'd lost touch with, something that is clearly unexpected. You don't get to specify the blessing (that comes later in Experiment #5), but you do need to give a clearly defined request and a concrete deadline. And as always, it helps to ask for help in recognizing your gift.

When Wendy tried this experiment, she received not just one, but two unexpected blessings. She got a dollar an hour raise (her boss called out of the blue) and her brother who lives out-of-state and never calls unless there's a death in the family phoned to volunteer to help her move, something he's never done in the six moves she's made before this one.

Results, depending on your consciousness, vary. Some people get something simple (Julie, for example, had a two-year-old boy she'd never seen before come sit beside her on a park bench. They smiled at each other like two long lost lovers) or it might be something pretty amazing. Eric was offered a free ski trip to Lake Tahoe.

Take note how you feel about asking the energy field for a blessing. Do you feel a bit antsy, wonder if you're being selfish, doubt whether or not it's appropriate to ask for something good? This feeling provides telling insight. Maybe you don't believe you deserve a gift. That thought sends signals to the energy field and affects its resonance. Perhaps you think it's only appropriate to ask for something you need. That signal, too, is being radioed to the energy field.

To do this experiment properly, you have to set aside skepticism. Not forever. Just for 48 short hours. All you have to do is spend 48 measly hours expecting to see God. Expect to see the Dude in living color. Expect it with your whole heart. Expect it with every ounce of your soul.

Like any good hypothesis, this one is falsifiable. If you don't hear from Cosmo K in 48 hours, well, feel free to write the guy off. Just think, you can be a total atheist for the rest of your life if the Dude lets you down.

LAB REPORT SHEET

The Principle:
The Dude Abides

The Theory:
There is a mind-boggling force that offers infinite love, tolerance, compassion, generosity, beauty, gentleness, joy, peace, and wisdom. And it's yours for the asking. Anytime, anywhere.

The Question:
Does the God force exist?

The Hypothesis:
If there's a 24/7 energy force equally available to everyone, I can access it at any time by simply paying attention. Furthermore, if I ask the force for a blessing, give it a specific time frame, and clear instructions, it'll send me a gift and say, "my pleasure."

Time required:
48 hours

Today's Date:

Time:

Deadline for receiving gift:

The Approach:
I hate to break it to ya, God, but folks are starting to talk. They're starting to wonder, "Is this guy for real?" I mean, really, like it'd be so much skin off your chin to come down here and call off this crazy hide-and-seek thing you've been playing. I'm giving you exactly 48 hours to make your presence known. I want a thumb's up, a clear sign, something that cannot be written off as coincidence.

I need to know if you really exist. I've been paying lip service to you for years now, but far as I can tell, I'm still pretty much the same person, just more frustrated. You've got exactly 48 hours to send me a sign that you are out there.

Research Notes:

THE VOLKSWAGEN JETTA PRINCIPLE

Whatever you focus on expands.

"Miracles are like pimples, because once you start looking for them you find more than you ever dreamed you'd see."
—Lemony Snicket

PREMISE:

One of the great spiritual principles is that whatever we devote our minds to expands. I like to call it the Volkswagen Jetta Principle.

Remember that new car you bought a few years ago? When you first decided it was the car of your dreams, it seemed like a really unique car. You figured you'd be the only one in town to proudly drive one. Well, by the time you finally got to the car dealership, read up on it in *Consumer Reports*, and decided on the price you needed to offer, you noticed that practically every eighth car was a Volkswagen Jetta or whatever car it was you wanted.

And that's what happens when we devote our minds to things we do not want. Lack, unhappiness, and danger are no more prevalent than a Volkswagen Jetta, but once we bring them into our consciousness, they sadly take over.

According to physicists, there's a Zero Point Field where every possibility exists. For example, there's the possibility you could be a ballerina, another that you could be a United States Senator. Still yet another possibility is bag lady in Haight-Ashbury. When it comes to the Zero Point Field, the possibilities are infinite.

Since I'm not a physicist and can barely pronounce the name David Boehm, let alone understand his theory of layered realities, I prefer to think of the Zero Point Field as a giant Wal-Mart with hundreds of thousands of products or possibilities. This is probably a good time to mention I'm not a fan of Wal-Mart, that I've never quite been able to forgive them for running my favorite corner pharmacy and fabric store out of town. But as a single mom on a budget, I do occasionally lower myself to shop there. And when I do, I know just where to find the fabric, the puzzles, the kids' shoes, all things I've been known to purchase. But most of the hundreds of thousands of products on the shelves I'm completely oblivious to. Why?

They're not what I'm looking for.

Doesn't mean they're not there. Doesn't mean they're not as "real" as the puzzles and shoes. It just means I'm not aware of them. For example, my daughter came home from school the other day with head lice. After panicking and briefly considering throwing myself off the nearest bridge, I finally concluded that I would provide a much better parental example by going in search of lice shampoo. Sure enough, on an aisle at Wal-Mart I'd walked down dozens, probably hundreds of times, was a complete selection of lice shampoo. Why had I never noticed it before?

It wasn't what I was looking for.

This simple, 48-hour experiment will prove that what you see in life is none other than what you look for. It will also prove that it's possible to find anything you look for. And most important, it will prove that by changing what you look for, you can radically change what shows up in your world.

THE CHAINS THAT BIND US

"Your wildest misperceptions, your weird imaginings, your blackest nightmares all mean nothing."
—Course in Miracles

A few years ago, a sweepstakes agency gave away one hundred free trips. Anywhere winners wanted to go. That meant lucky winners could fly to Paris to see the Eiffel Tower or jet to Australia and climb Ayers rock or sail to a beach in the Caribbean islands. And you know what? Ninety-five percent of the winners picked a destination within four hours of their home. Four hours!

That contest pretty much sums up the human condition. So much is out there, but most of us choose to stay within four hours of our "comfort zones." We refuse to budge, even when there's ample evidence we're missing out on big things.

Without being truly conscious of it, we spend most of our waking hours immersed in the comfort zone of negativity. The pull of the negative is so strong that we navigate our entire days by jumping from one depressing thought to another: I overslept again, this war is unconscionable, the economy is in shambles, gas is expensive, my boss or my kid or my fill-in-the-blank is driving me crazy.

Negativity and fear start the minute we're born: "It's a scary world out there, Jimmy. Don't you dare talk to strangers. Don't you dare sing that silly song at the grocery store. Someone might hear."

We learn to limit. We learn to believe in scarcity. We learn that our natural inclination to love and to create and to dance is impractical and crazy.

Our parents think it's their sworn duty to teach us to be careful, to be responsible, to act like adults. And if for some reason we're lucky enough to get parents who don't dispense these lessons, our culture quickly indoctrinates us into believing that collecting material things is our purpose in life and that the only way to get those goodies is to put our proverbial snouts to the grindstone. By the time we're in grade school, we're already masters at competition, old pros at living in scarcity and fear.

But guess what? It's all a big ruse, a big ploy to keep Cosmo K's infinite beauty and unending goodness from our awareness. As the Course in Miracles clearly states. "Once you develop a thought system of any kind, you live by it and teach it." Once you form a belief, you attach all your senses and all your life to its survival.

Physicists call this phenomenon "collapse of the wave." Infinite numbers of quantum particles are out in the universal field dancing around, spreading out in waves. The moment someone looks at these energy waves they solidify like gelatin in the refrigerator. Your observing is what makes them appear solid, real, material.

Remember Snow White when she's lying on the forest floor crying? She feels as if all these eyes are staring at her. And indeed all these forest creatures are skittering and scampering about. But the moment she raises her head to look, all the cute little birds, squirrels, and deer dive behind trees. All she can see is a solid, non-moving forest.

In reality, our universe is a moving, scampering energy field with infinite possibilities, but because our eyes have locked in on problem mode, that's what appears to be reality.

IT SURE LOOKS LIKE REALITY.
OR YOU'LL SEE IT WHEN YOU BELIEVE IT.

"You will not break loose until you realize that you
yourself forge the chains that bind you."
—Arten in *The Disappearance of the Universe*

In 1970, Colin Blakemore and G.F. Cooper, scientists at Cambridge University, did a fascinating experiment with kittens. This must have been before animal rights activists got vocal,
because what they did was take a litter of kittens and deprive them of light. Except for once
a day, for just an hour or two, the scientists beamed in just enough lights for the kittens to
see a couple vertical black and white stripes. That's it. A couple hours, a couple stripes. Now
I don't know whether their consciences finally got the better of them or whether PETA started breathing down their neck, but after several months they figured they better release the
kittens from the dark. What they discovered was the kittens' cortical cells that favored non-
vertical orientation had gone into hibernation. They could no longer make out vertical lines.
They literally bumped into horizontal ropes stretched out in front of them.

Their perceptions were influenced by what they had been conditioned to see. As thinking beings, we continually try to make sense of our world. Sounds like a good thing, right?
Except that any piece of information that doesn't quite fit with our beliefs, we alter without
even noticing. We knead and we squeeze until everything finally fits into the tight box of our
limited belief system.

We think what we perceive with our senses is true, but the fact I will keep banging you over the head with is it's only one half of one millionth of a percent of what's possible.

At the base of the brain stem, about the size of a gumdrop, is a group of cells whose job is to sort and evaluate incoming data. This control center, known as the reticular activating system (RAS), has the job of sending what it thinks is urgent to the active part of the brain and to steer the non-urgent stuff to the back. But as it's organizing, it's also busy interpreting, drawing inferences, and filtering out anything that doesn't jive with what we believe.

In other words, we rehearse ahead of time the world we want to see. Too bad we all picked up the wrong script.

As much as I want to start passing out scripts, I'm going to tell you a story instead. A Native American grandfather was talking to his young grandson. He tells the boy about two wolves who are fighting a great battle inside him. The first is the wolf of peace, love, and kindness. The other is the wolf of fear, greed, and hatred. "Which wolf will win, grandfather?" asks the young boy. "Whichever one I feed, son, whichever one I feed."

ANECDOTAL EVIDENCE:

"Toto, I don't think we're in Kansas anymore."
—Dorothy in *The Wizard of Oz*

You've probably never heard of Peter and Eileen Caddy. But I'll bet the name Findhorn rings a bell. Remember that garden in Scotland where they grew cabbages big enough to knock over a postal truck? Well, Peter and Eileen Caddy are the folks who grew those 40-pound cabbages (Keep in mind that the average cabbage is four pounds, five ounces) and they did it by focusing their thoughts on spiritual truth.

They certainly didn't have anything else going for them. In fact, when the Caddys, their three sons, and Dorothy Maclean moved into the trailer on that wind-blown peninsula jutting out into the North Sea, the land could best be described as dead and profitless. Nobody in their right mind would have chosen it as a spot to grow anything, let alone a garden. The soil—if you could call it that—consisted of rocks and sand, the wind gales were strong enough to knock over the average second grader, and their-less-than-Better-Homes-locale was smack dab between a garbage dump and a dilapidated garage.

But by focusing on a higher truth, they created a garden that can only be described as miraculous. Although it was the 40-pound cabbages that got all the publicity, the Caddys also grew 65 other types of vegetables, 21 kinds of fruits, and 42 different herbs. And this is before they started adding flowers.

I know what you're thinking: rich compost and good organic husbandry. But the truth is the Caddy's soil was so pathetic that the county extension agent said even compost couldn't help. At the time, they started their experiment in higher consciousness, the Caddys had never gardened, nor did they have money to invest in gardening supplies. They were broke—to put it mildly. Peter, who had managed a successful four-star hotel, had been laid off and the six of them were living on unemployment that amounted to roughly $20 a week.

No, they started growing vegetables for one reason. They thought it might be a nice gesture to feed their three growing boys. But as they began aligning their consciousness with spiritual truth and nothing else, all sorts of strange things started happening. Straw bales started falling off passing trucks just in time to mulch. Leftover bags of cement mix mysteriously showed up in a neighbor's trash bin just in time to pour a patio. Their plants, while the crops of their neighbors suffered, became resistant to diseases and pests. Eventually, people started flocking to the Caddys garden and, today, Findhorn is a prosperous spiritual community that attracts 14,000 seekers every year.

As Peter says, "You can bring about anything by your thoughts. Align yourself with God consciousness and you can bring about truth in material form. What you think, you create."

There is no power on earth that can cut you off from God's truth love, peace, joy, abundance, happiness, beauty, and expansion except your own consciousness.

METHOD:

"With those eyes, my bonny lad, I'm afraid you'll never see it."
—Johnny Depp as J.M. Barrie in *Finding Neverland*

For the next 48 hours (that's all, a pain-free, two-day commitment. You are free to go back to your miserable life as soon as this experiment is over), you are going to actively look for certain things. And just like sixth graders who start out dissecting worms, not human bodies, you're going to begin with something simple—green cars. Okay, if you insist, you can pick another color. Sunset beige, for example. For the first 24 hours of the experiment, you're going to make the following conscious intention. "I hereby intend for the next day of my life to look for . . . okay, you win . . . sunset beige vehicles." Again, you don't have to do anything special. Just keep your eyes open. Just make the intention. And then simply notice if your conscious awareness has made a difference in the number of sunset beige cars you see.

On day two, during the following 24-hour period, you're going to make the intention to see butterflies. I don't care if it's the middle of winter. Make the intention. Jeanette tried the experiment in January in the upper peninsula of Michigan and found butterflies on stationery, on a paper cup at her daughter's friend's birthday party. The point is don't let your previous conditioning influence you in any way. Just open your mind and look, consciously actively look—as if you had misplaced your car keys.

LAB REPORT SHEET

The Principle:
The Volkswagen Jetta Principle

The Theory:
Whatever you focus on expands.

The Question:
Do I really see only what I expect to see?

The Hypothesis:
If I decide to look for sunset beige cars and butterflies, I will find them.

Time required:
48 hours

Today's Date:

Time:

The Approach:
According to this crazy Pam Grout girl, the world out there reflects what I want to see. She says that it's nothing but my own illusions that keep me from experiencing peace, joy, and love. So even though I suspect she's cracked, today, I'm going to look for sunset beige cars. Tomorrow, I'll go butterfly watching.

a. Number of sunset beige cars observed

b. Number of butterflies observed

Research Notes:

Research Notes Continued:

THE ALBY EINSTEIN PRINCIPLE

You are a field of energy in an even bigger field of energy.

"It's right underneath your fingers, baby. That's all you have to understand—everything is right underneath your fingers."

—Ray Charles

PREMISE:

I'm not going to bore you with an entire text on quantum physics. I've read dozens and, believe me, they're not pretty. But there are a couple rumors going around that must be squashed before we go any further.

For starters, who you think you are is not who you really are.

You actually bought the idea that you're nothing but a physical body with flesh and bones, organs, bad breath, and occasional gas. You actually fell for the con job that you're separate from all the other 6 billion bodies out there on Planet Earth.

You think you have a limited life, something like 60 or 70 years and then you wrinkle up, get rheumatism and keel over. Kabloom! It's all over. But this isn't anymore true than that dream you had last night about the tall blonde.

Your body is an imposter, a tiny fraction of who you really are. Ninety-nine percent of who you are is invisible and untouchable. This body that I think is Pam Grout—this 5'10", skinny woman with perpetual complexion problems—is just a speck of who I really am, no more the real me than those two-month-old baby pictures where I'm wearing the embarrassing pink bonnet.

Don't feel bad if you've fallen for the trap that you, your body, and the world around you is mere matter. It's not easy standing on the brink of a revolution. These new ideas that scientists are finally starting to take seriously are challenging everything we believe about how our world works and how we define ourselves.

THE WHOLE TRUTH AND NOTHING BUT THE TRUTH

"I knew it. I knew it. Well, not in the sense of having the slightest idea,
but I knew there was something I didn't know."
—Willow, from *Buffy, the Vampire Slayer*

What Einstein discovered and what that famous equation $E=mc^2$ means is that mass and energy are basically two forms of the same thing. Energy is liberated matter and matter is energy waiting to happen.

There is a huge amount of energy—a preposterously huge amount—trapped in every living thing. Let's make the assumption that you're an average size human being. What that means, in Albert Einstein's world, is that you can contain no less than 7×10 to the 18th joules of potential energy. That may not mean much now, but let's assume you want to make a point. If you were a bit more cunning and knew how to liberate this energy, you could use it to explode yourself with the force of thirty very large hydrogen bombs.

In other words, the material world is nothing but dense energy patterns. Scientists put all these sub-sub atomic particles into a particle accelerator, collided them, and ultimately discovered that there is no particle at the source. The source is pure unbounded energy vibrating so fast it defies measurement and observation. So, despite how it looks to the naked eye, you are energy.

In fact, nothing in the world is actually solid. Not you, not this book, not the chair you're sitting on. Break the solid world down to its tiniest components and you'll find dancing particles and empty space. It only looks solid because the energy is vibrating at a little less than the speed of light.

That's what energy is—vibrating particles, so that means you, this book, and the chair are actually vibrating.

Energy is a pretty nebulous thing. You can't see it, scratch it, or take it out to dinner. But you can (and do every day) influence how it flows through you. And since it's the building block of everything in the universe that's a powerful thing.

At each moment, you mold and shape the energy by your consciousness. You do this with every thought, every intention, every action. How you feel, what you think, how you believe, what you value, and how you live your life affects how the energy flows through you. To put it in simplest terms, it affects how you vibrate.

And how you vibrate affects what you pull in from the interlocking, interbalancing, ever-moving energy field in which you swim. You pull out of this field and into your world anything that happens to be vibrating on the same frequency or wavelength.

Let's say you're feeling excited, joyful, and grateful. Those emotions send out high frequency vibrations that magnetize more things to be excited, joyful, and grateful about. Anything with the same high frequency will cavort on over to your energy field.

On the other hand, if you're scared, guilt-ridden, and convinced there's a terrorist around every corner, you're sending out low frequency vibrations that will attract ugly things into your life.

We always attract our vibrational match. We are the initiators of the vibrations, therefore, the magnets, the cause.

It works the same as a tuning fork. Ding a tuning fork in a room filled with tuning forks calibrated to different pitches, and only the ones calibrated to the same frequency will ding too. And they'll ding all the way across the Metrodome. Like forces attract: it's a classic rule of physics.

THERE IS NO YOU AND THEM.

"Anyone who is not shocked by physics has not understood it."
—Niels Bohr

As if you didn't already have enough weirdness to contend with, I'm going to throw in one more tiny detail. Everything in the physical world, as we know it, is connected to everything in the physical world. You are attached and engaged to one underlying universal energy field. "The field," as Daddy Einstein said, "is the only reality."

Things appear separate because they're vibrating at different wave lengths same as the note "C" vibrates at a different wave length than "B-Flat." Each of these vibrations create a strand in the electromagnetic field which in turns instructs energy where to go and what to do.

This pulsating energy field is the central engine of your being and your consciousness. Where is this field? There's no place it's not. Everything in the universe is hooked up to the energy field, all life forms whether Siberian Tigers, houseplants, or icebergs. Your intelligence, creativity, and imagination interact with this magnificent and complex energy field.

If you were in the Manhattan Macy's at 4 PM, August 14, 2003, you probably thought the power going out was an isolated event. For all you knew, a taxi on 34th Street ran into a light pole and cut the lines. But after the power finally came back on so you could listen to the news again, you discovered that the blackout at Macy's was connected to blackouts in eight states and the Canadian province of Ontario. One tiny little malfunctioning monitoring tool in one tiny little plant in Ohio caused 263 power plants to screech to a halt.

We may look like separate bodies with separate ideas, but we are all just one big pulsating, vibrating field of consciousness.

ANECDOTAL EVIDENCE:

"It ain't what you don't know that gets you into trouble. It's what you know for sure that just ain't so."
—Mark Twain

Edwine Gaines is one of my favorite Unity ministers. She's funny, she's wise, and she knows how spiritual principles work. She travels the country giving prosperity seminars, teaching people how to live more abundant, God-centered lives.

But like the rest of us, Edwine had to learn about spiritual principles through trial and error. She tells a hilarious story about her "first big demonstration." A demonstration, according to Unitics (that's folks who hang out at Unity churches) is when you pull something you want or need out of thin air—more or less.

At the time of Edwine's first demonstration, she was relatively new to spiritual principles. She was what you could politely call broke. As she says, "I didn't have two dimes to rub together."

But she heard this crazy rumor that not only did God like her, but that he wanted to open the gates of heaven and pour out his blessings—if she simply learned how to direct her energy. But first she had to know what she wanted and when she wanted it.

That was easy. Wasn't 15 minutes before Edwine had a whole yellow legal pad filled with her desires—new green shoes, new male partner, new car, etc.

Edwine also decided she wanted a week's vacation to Mexico City. She'd never been there, but she figured it would be a great place to practice her Spanish. Plus she'd always wanted to see the Pyramid of the Sun, the Pyramid of the Moon, Diego Rivera's paintings, and the Aztec calendar.

She didn't have any money for the trip so writing it down was a "bit of a joke." But she figured, "What the heck!" She even went down to a travel agent, looked at brochures, and made a tentative reservation for three months, the date she decided she wanted to travel.

"I figured the worst that could happen is I'd be embarrassed in front of the travel agent when I'm not able to pay," Edwine says.

"That's only because you don't feel rich," her teacher said. "You're not vibrating as a rich person. You need to go out and do something to make yourself feel rich"

Edwine decided her biggest challenge was the grocery store.

"I was one of those people who bought the bare minimum—beans, cornbread, flour, the basics," she says. "I didn't dare splurge on any of that foo-foo stuff. Nothing like bubble bath. I had a budget."

So next time, she's at the grocery store, she decides to saunter over to the gourmet counter. Just for a gander.

"I noticed this bottle of olives stuffed with almonds," Edwine says. "I took one look at that and just knew that was what rich people ate."

So she bought it, took her groceries home, and called her friend, Lana.

"Lana, I'm coming over. We're going to sit by your pool, we're going to get out your new crystal wine glasses, and drink that bottle of wine you just bought. We're going to eat the olives I just splurged on, and we're going to pretend we're on an exotic vacation in Mexico City."

"Say what?" Lana said.

But Lana agreed to play along. And sure enough, they sat by Lana's pool, drinking wine, eating olives, laughing, and pretending to be vacationing in Mexico City.

"Well, darling, which pyramid should we visit tomorrow?" Edwine would ask. "Or maybe you'd rather go to the beach."

And then Lana would answer, "Let's do both and after that we can walk through the marketplace and listen to mariachis."

"We had so much fun," Edwine says. "That Lana decided she wanted to go to Mexico City, too."

The next day, Lana went down to the same travel agency and made her reservations. Within a week, Lana's mom called her and said, "Hey, guess what? I'd like to pay for that ticket to Mexico City."

"And I was the one doing the affirmations," Edwine jokes.

A few weeks later, the travel agent calls Edwine and informs her that unless she comes down today to pay for her tickets, she was going to have to let them go.

"Okay, I'll be right there," Edwine said to the travel agent, even though she felt like the little old lady with the bare cupboards and the dog without a bone. "I got in my car and decided it was time I had a severe talking to with God."

"God," I said. "Now, I've done everything I know how to do here. I've made my list. I've done my affirmations. I've been acting rich. The way I figure it, the rest is up to you. And, big guy, since this travel agent is calling, I'm going to go ahead and go on down and that money better be there."

On the way to the travel agency, she gets a hunch to stop by her mom's house.

"Now I know myself well enough to know that I was probably thinking that if I told my mom about Lana's mom buying her ticket maybe she'd agree to buy my ticket," Edwine admits.

She goes into her mom's house, acts just as sweet as can be, and tells her mom about this vacation that she and Lana cooked up.

She finishes her story, looks up at her mom and says, "And you know what? Lana's mom even agreed to pay for Lana's ticket. Isn't that wonderful?"

"That is wonderful," Edwine's mom said. "What are you going to do?"

Discouraged, Edwine starts to walk out the door when her mom asks if she'd be kind enough to run out and get her mail. Her mom's house had a long driveway, so Edwine walks out the to the mailbox, kicking at stones and cursing under her breath.

On the way back, Edwine decides to take a little look-see through her mom's mail. She notices a letter addressed to her.

"Now understand, I hadn't lived at my mom's house for 15 years and hadn't received mail there for 15 years," she says.

Edwine, not having a clue who this person was on the return address, rips opens the envelope. Lo and behold, there's a letter from an old roommate, who had gotten married since she and Edwine had lived together 15 years earlier. At the time, they were both young, poor, and forced to decorate with what Edwine calls, "Early Salvation Army."

Not three months after they moved in, Edwine landed a job teaching overseas and left the roommate, the apartment, and the used furniture behind.

Here's what the letter said:

> Dear Edwine:
>
> I was looking through the Houston phone book the other day and saw your parent's address. I wanted to tell you that I've gotten married and moved into a nice, new house with my new husband. We furnished our house with all new furniture,

so I sold all that furniture we bought 15 years ago. Turns out, would you believe it? That some of it was pretty valuable. I didn't feel right keeping all the money since we had worked so hard to furnish that place. Please find a check for your half of the money."

"And do you know?" says Edwine. "It was the exact amount I needed to pay for my ticket to the penny plus $100 for spending money."

THE METHOD

"The western scientific community, and actually all of us, are in a difficult spot, because in order to maintain our current mode of being, we must ignore a tremendous amount of information."
—Cleve Backster

Even though this principle is one of the cornerstone spiritual principles (remember spiritual just means the opposite of material), it actually first came to light, not in a church, but in a physics lab. Yes, it was scientists who first discovered that, despite all appearances to the contrary, human beings are not matter, but continually moving waves of energy.

In this experiment you're going to prove that your thoughts and feelings also create energy waves. Here's what you do: Get two wire coat hangers, easy to obtain in most any coat closet. Untwist the neck of each hanger until you've got just two straight wires. These are your Einstein wands. Or they will be when you shape them into an "L", about twelve-inches long for the main part and five-inches for the handle. Cut a plastic straw, (you can score one free of charge at any McDonald's), place it around the handle (it'll make your wand swing easily), and bend the bottom of the hanger to hold the straw in place.

Now, pretend you're a double-fisted, gun-swinging Matt Dillon with the wands held chest high and about ten-inches from the body. They'll flap all over the place at first (like I said, you're an ongoing river of energy), so give them a few minutes to settle down. Once they've stopped flapping, you're ready to begin the experiment.

With your eyes straight ahead, recall with feeling some very unpleasant event from your past. Depending on the intensity of your emotion, the wands will either stay straight ahead (weak intensity) or will point inward, tip to tip. The wands are following the electromagnetic bands around your body which have contracted as a result of the negative frequency generated by your unpleasant thought and emotions.

Now make your frequencies turn positive, by thinking about something loving or joyous. The wands will now expand outward as your energy field expands to your positive energy flow.

Okay, now keep your eyes straight ahead, but focus your attention on an object to your far right or far left and watch your wands follow your thoughts. The more you play with this, the more adept you'll become at feeling the vibrational shift as you change from one frequency to another.

LAB REPORT SHEET

The Principle:
The Alby Einstein Principle

The Theory:
You are a field of energy in an even bigger field of energy.

The Question:
Could it really be true that I'm made up of energy?

The Hypothesis:
If I am energy, I can direct my energy.

Time required:
Two hours of experimentation.

Today's Date:

Time:

Research Notes:

Research Notes Continued:

EXPERIMENT # 4:

THE DONALD TRUMP PRINCIPLE

The universe is limitless, abundant, and strangely accommodating.

"What if this powerful force was used to uplift people rather than keep them trapped in the corporate and religious food chain?"

—Mark Vicente

PREMISE:

This experiment will dispel the myth that life sucks and then you die. Most of us, whether we admit it or not, believe life is hard. We believe there's only so much to go around— whether we're talking money, time, or popcorn at the Multiplex Cinema. Even people with Maseratis in their garage spend way too much time figuring out how to get more.

Why? Because they mistakenly believe there's "not enough." Even billionaires, even people with an overabundance of resources, live under the oppressive spell of "there's not enough."

A friend of mine was interviewing the wealthy owner of a successful business whose company was launching a new product. Noticing the rabid dollar signs in his eyes, she asked him if there was a profit margin, a success index, a dollar amount of some kind that he would consider "enough." The business owner stopped for a second, sighed, and gave this reply, "Man, you just don't get it. There is never enough."

It's like that game "musical chairs." Everyone's worried that when the music stops, they'll be the one without a place to sit.

Converse to everything you know, the Donald Trump experiment proposes that there is a natural law of abundance and that everything's okay, you can relax. For just 48 short hours, you're going to set aside your normal thinking patterns and allow them to be superceded by the remote possibility that there might be enough. For everyone.

SOMETHING IS WRONG WITH THIS PICTURE

"If you think there's a bogeyman, turn on the light."
–Dorothy Thompson

Scarcity and lack is our default setting, the unquestioned condition that defines our life.

The mantra "there's not enough" starts first thing every morning with the alarm.

"Ah, shit, I didn't get enough z's."

Before we even sit up, before we even squeeze our feet into our bunny slippers, we're already bemoaning lack. When we finally do get up, it's, "Now I don't have enough time to get ready."

And from there it goes down hill.

We spend large chunks of our energy worrying and complaining about not getting enough. We don't have enough time. We don't get enough exercise or fiber or vitamin E. Our paychecks aren't big enough. Our weekends aren't long enough. We ourselves, poor things, are not thin enough, not smart enough, not educated enough.

It never even occurs to us to examine whether or not this "not enough" mantra is true. It's so engrained in us that it shapes our deepest sense of who we are. Being deficient has become the lens through which we experience every facet of our life.

It's why we take jobs that don't satisfy us. It's why we stay in unfulfilling relationships. It's why we keep going back to the buffet line long after our appetites have been filled which could be, duh!, why we have a weight problem in this country. It's why big, powerful countries like say, us, pick on less fortunate countries. It's why corporations cut corners for the sake of profit.

It's why we've created systems and institutions to control access to resources (oil anyone?) we perceive as valuable and limited. If we weren't so worried about not having enough, we could relax and use the resources we do have to develop alternative sources of energy, energy, I hasten to point out, like the sun or the wind that will never run out.

The "not enough" fiction drives us to do things we're not proud of, things that compromise our highest ideals, things that lay waste to the natural world, things that separate us from God. And once we define ourselves as deficient, all our energy gets sucked into making sure we're not the one being left out, not the one losing ground to the "other guy."

But here's the deal. It's all a big, fat, unfortunate lie. There is enough. For everyone. We live in a big, bounteous universe and if we can just get over our this unfounded fear of there not being enough, we can stop hoarding resources (c'mon, who really needs 89 pairs of shoes?) and free up our energy to make sure all of us get what we need.

Right now, with the resources already at your disposal (you don't have to get a new job or find a new relationship or even start a time-consuming new yoga practice), you can begin to recognize and lead a rich and meaningful life. And the best part is you can quit working so damned hard. Take it easy for a change. You don't have to do everything yourself. Would it kill you to try depending on "The Dude"?

ANECDOTAL EVIDENCE:

"You can never get enough of what you don't really need."
—Eric Hoffer, mid-20th century philosopher

The United States is the richest country in the world, but if you look at the UN's human development index that ranks quality of life, America is way down the list. And dropping every year. Americans consume 75 percent more than Europeans (who have smaller homes, rely on public transportation, and have compact, efficient appliances), but Europeans enjoy a 25 percent higher quality of life.

Even without statistics, it's pretty easy to observe that people in the western world feel deficient in some way. Why else would they be buying all these self-help books, taking antidepressants, and mindlessly shopping for things they don't need? We're rich beyond measure, but we feel strapped, scared, always on guard.

Sure, we call ourselves an abundant society, but in many ways it's nothing but an illusion, a ruse, thanks to the ever present "there's not enough" mantra. We're too busy playing musical chairs, running faster and faster around that illusory circle of shrinking chairs.

The Chumash Indians, who lived for thousands of years on the central coast of California, enjoyed what I would call a rich and prosperous life. They lived in small, close-knit villages, used the natural resources around them to make canoes, arrows, and medicines. They regularly dined on more than 150 kinds of seafood, honeydew melons, and pine nuts. They made fur blankets, soapstone pots decorated with shells, and extraordinary baskets, so tightly woven they could hold water. And almost every day, the Chumash played games, danced, sang lullabies to their children, and enjoyed a cleansing sweat in the village apu'yik.

Nowadays, we call that type of lifestyle "subsistence." We look down upon it as a hard-scrabble existence. But what I'd like to suggest is that the Chumash, unlike us, lived in an economy of abundance. To the Chumash, there was always enough. Not too much. Not too little. Enough. Most important, there was enough time for things that matter—relationships, delicious food, art, games, and rest.

METHOD:

"If your only tool is a hammer, you tend to see every problem as a nail."
—Abraham Maslow

In this experiment, we hold the Dude to that guarantee he made in the New Testament. Remember He promised that if we'd just quit worrying, we'd be clothed, fed, and taken better care of than the lilies of the field? Well, for the next 48 hours, we're going to leave our wallets at home. And, yes, that means credit cards, too. We're going to put our trust in the goodness of the universe. Again, go on about your normal business, keep your regular schedule, your job, your commitments. The only difference is that unlike that American Express commercial, you're going to leave home without it.

There is one more rule: Don't tell anyone about your experiment.

If this experiment strikes terror in your heart, just remember that it took eight weeks for

Bobby Sands, the IRA activist, to die from a hunger strike. I'm just pulling your leg, not that Sands died from a hunger strike, but that you are putting your life in any kind of peril. Besides, before Sands kicked the bucket, he was elected Irish Republican MP.

On second thought, I'd rather tell you the story of Paramahansa Yogananda. When he was 15, he was sent to the Indian city of Brindaban with nary a rupee. He had been yammering to his family about wanting to quit school and devote his life to God. His brother, a stolid accountant, decided to pull a fast one on his pious pipsqueak brother. "Okay," he challenged him, "You wanna do God's work, fine. But let's forget about your inheritance. If you wanna depend on God, I insist you depend on Him for everything. What do you say we put your vaunted philosophy to a test in the tangible world?"

Ananta, the sermonizing elder brother made this proposal. "I'll buy you a one-way ticket to Brindaban. It's where Lord Krishna first displayed his glories, so it'll be a good place for you to start. You spend the day there. Take no money. No food. You're not allowed to beg. Yet you can't go without food or transportation. Furthermore, you're not allowed to reveal your predicament to anyone. If you return to my bungalow before midnight without breaking any of these rules, I'll not only give you my blessing, but I'll become your first initiate."

Ananta undoubtedly smirked as he sent his penniless brother and a friend off to the strange city they'd never visited, but not before searching both of them for a hidden hoard.

The friend, lacking the young yogi's faith, was nervous—almost as nervous as you probably are in contemplating this next experiment.

"Shouldn't we take a couple rupees just as a safeguard?" he pleaded. "At least then we'll have money to telegraph you in case of misfortune. There's something reassuring about the clink of coins."

Paramahansa rebuked his friend, refusing to proceed with the test if he took any "safeguard."

As the train rumbled towards the holy city, the friend started whining. "I'm really getting hungry. Why did you talk me into this?"

Right before the last stop, two men stepped into their compartment, began joking with the young boys. When the train pulled to a stop, the two men linked arms with the boys and led them into a horse cab.

Well, long story short, they ended up at an ashram, taking the place of two princes who, at the last minute, had to cancel their lunch plans. Not only were they served a 30-course meal, while being fanned by a hostess, but they visited Madanamohana Temple and other Krishna shrines, were given train tickets back to Agra, and fed the finest of Indian sweetmeats for dinner.

Was Ananta ever surprised when, at a few minutes before midnight, the young yogi walks into his home with piles of rupee notes and bursting with stories. His brother, as promised, insisted on receiving spiritual initiation that very evening.

LAB REPORT SHEET

The Principle:
The Donald Trump Principle

The Theory:
The universe is limitless, abundant, and strangely accommodating.

The Question:
Is it possible I worry too much and that life really will take care of me?

The Hypothesis:
If I change my outlook and refuse to play the game, I will discover an unending supply of good. Furthermore, if I let the universe take care of me, it will.

Time required:
48 hours

Today's Date:

Time:

The Approach:
C'mon God, I though you were all-seeing? Have you had a look in my pocketbook lately? Alright, already, I'll give it a try. For just 48 hours. Forty-eight hours in which I'm going to take you up on that little offer you made about the lilies of the field. I'm not going to depend on my own resources at all for the next few days. I have no idea how you're going to do it. I just know that it's now your job.

I guess you could call this your big chance, as Cuba Gooding Jr. would say to "show me the money."

Research Notes:

Research Notes Continued:

THE ABRACADABRA PRINCIPLE

Thoughts held in mind create after their kind.

"I can manipulate the external influences in my life as surely as I can make a baby cry by grinning."

—Augusten Burroughs

PREMISE:

When I first heard that thoughts could bring material goods into my life, I did what any intelligent, thinking person would do. I scoffed. But I also decided to give it a try. What could it hurt to conduct a secret experiment?

Andrea, my teacher, said to write down three things I wanted. That's all. I didn't have to zap them out of thin air. I didn't have to work out a budget. I just had to make a list. What the heck. I want a bicycle, a computer, and a piano.

Within two weeks, I had a beautiful red mountain bike and an IBM PC Junior. The piano took a little bit longer. But six years ago, my friend Wendy, who was moving to Maryland, called and told me if I'd come get it, I could have her beautiful, brown cherry Kimball. My daughter, who desperately wants to quit piano lessons, has been cursing me ever since.

Yes, this is the chapter you've all been waiting for. The chapter on how to manifest material things. It's the spiritual principle that attracts would-be believers like 15-year-old males to Cameron Diaz.

Let me guess. At some point in your life, you've read *Think and Grow Rich, The Magic of Believing, The Power of Positive Thinking,* or some combination thereof. As old and crotchety as these books might be, there's a reason they are still in print. They speak of a universal truth. *If you know what you want, you can have it.*

My friend, Chris . . . okay, most of my friends . . . think this principle employs magic, some mysterious ju-ju that might work for some people, but not others, say them. But it's not anymore complicated than walking from New Orleans to Biloxi, Mississippi once you have the right map. Let's say New Orleans is what you have now—a beat-up '94 Escort, a job you can't stand, and a lot of weekends watching videos by yourself. Biloxi, where you really want to be, is a shiny new Jaguar, a high-paying job that utilizes and appreciates your greatest strengths, and weekends watching videos with an astoundingly hot specimen of the opposite sex.

So, how do you get there? You start focusing on Biloxi. You forget that New Orleans and your beat-up '94 Escort even exist. And you remember that at every moment, you're either heading towards Biloxi or you're doubling back towards New Orleans. Every thought is a step in one direction or the other. Thoughts that take you back to New Orleans are "Good jobs and hot dates are not that available" or the even more popular, "Good jobs and hot dates are available, but not for the likes of me."

Thoughts that move you towards Biloxi go something like this: "That new job is going to be so amazing." and "Man, is this person sitting next to me on my couch ever so fine." The more energy and excitement you invest, the quicker you'll get there.

Some people get stirred up, take a few steps towards their desires, panic, and turn right back around towards New Orleans. Others leave the New Orleans city limits, walk for a spell, take a rest to look around, and then get pissed because it doesn't look like Biloxi.

Of course, it doesn't look like Biloxi. You're not there yet. You're still seeing countryside that's just outside New Orleans, stuff you're going to have to pass to get to Biloxi. But you've left New Orleans. Say a cheer and keep focusing. Whatever you do, don't stop walking. The only way to reach the sweet, champagne-drenched finish line of where you want to be is to keep your nose pointed in that direction. Do not turn around and look back. New Orleans is history. Stay focused on . . . did I mention Biloxi?

Other menacing distractions: At first, you'll feel glorious about this new heroic endeavor. You'll be astonished at how easy it is for you to stay focused on the beautiful city of Biloxi. You'll be laughing and skipping and enjoying the vistas. But, inevitably, your thoughts will get sore, they'll get bored with the new routine, and they'll want to head back towards New Orleans—you know, just for a quick visit, just one cup of tea. You start spending less and less time on Biloxi and more and more time on why the whole endeavor is futile. Maybe you should put it out of its misery before it's old enough to remember where you live.

But don't do it. Just keep walking, keep focusing on Biloxi.

At the risk of being anal, I want to make it clear that the New Orleans-Biloxi example is only a metaphor. When it comes to manifesting, there's no real physical work involved. It's all about training your mind, that incorrigible slacker.

It sounds pie-in-the-sky, I know. But I've seen it happen time and time again. Getting to Biloxi doesn't take any particular gift. It just takes willingness to keep walking. And focus large enough to wound a moose.

I always think of a magician pulling a scarf through a hole. If you can just grab a hold of one tiny end, you can pull it all the way through. That's all it takes—one itty-bitty end. Decide you want it and keep focusing until you've pulled it all the way through.

What can you manifest? Pretty much anything you've ever seen, heard, or experienced. The world basically is your Sears and D̲ ̲ ̲uck catalog. If you've seen it . . . or even if you can imagine it, just grab an end and start walking towards Biloxi.

Maybe I should be more specific. Don's Biloxi was a Martin guitar. Martin guitars start at $1100, and while he didn't have the ready cash, Don made the intention to own a Martin guitar. He didn't do a damned thing, just kept believing (focusing on that moose) that someday, somehow he'd get one. A few months, nearly a year later, he gets a message from his mom.

"Your dad just picked up an old guitar at a garage sale for $5. It can be a toy for Daisy."

Well, that old toy for Daisy was a rare 1943 Martin 000-28, one of only 100 made, the same guitar Eric Clapton plays, worth somewhere in the neighborhood of $20,000. It seems Daisy will have to wait and inherit the guitar in Don's will.

I also need to bring up this principle's nickname—the Statue of Liberty principle. Even though this principle is the beacon that represents everything people think they want—vacations to Jamaica, second homes in Maui, etc.—it's actually way down on Maslow's hierarchy. It's on the first, maybe second rung. You need to get this principle down, of course, so you can take your mind off material worries, so you can know the truth about who you are, but none of this stuff is what you really want. Not really. That's why I've nicknamed it the Statue of Liberty principle.

If you live in New York, you have no pressing need to visit Lady Liberty every day. You're confident she's there when you need here, but you're also free to move around lightly. All the material stuff just bogs you down. Jesus could never have brought Lazarus back to life and multiplied all those fishes and loaves if he'd have been responsible for a big home in

Malibu. That said, I do not want to make you feel guilty for wanting a big home in Malibu. There is not one thing wrong with a big home in Malibu. Or anything else you want. Do not feel guilty. Want it. Walk towards it with all your heart and might. Just know there are higher rungs. And know that most people hoard material stuff out of fear. And fear, after all, is what we're attempting to move away from.

GOOD, GOOD, GOOD, GOOD VIBRATIONS

"Every day, you are signaled and summoned to embark on a journey beyond the boundaries of all you have ever known. You need only relinquish your fears, open your heart, and begin."
—Bob Savino

Okay, just say it. "How can something as simple as a thought influence the world?" Let me just say that a hundred years ago nobody would have believed songs sung by a bunch of *American Idol* contestants could pass through brick, glass, wood, and steel to get from a transmitter tower to your television set either. Nobody would have believed a cell phone no bigger than an ear of corn would allow you to talk to your sister 2000 miles away.

Your thoughts, like the 289 TV channels, like your voice on the cell phone, are vibrational waves.

When you hear Eminem rapping about his daughter Hailey, your eardrum is catching a vibrational sound wave. When you see J. Lo's barely-there green dress, you're seeing patterns of vibrational light waves.

And that's what your thoughts are—vibrational waves that interact and influence the force field.

Thought is pure energy. Every thought you have, have ever had, or ever will have creates a vibration that goes out into the force field extending forever. These vibrations meet other vibrations, crisscrossing in an incredible maze of energy. Get enough energy together and it clumps into matter. Remember what Einstein said—matter is formed out of energy.

People think Jesus is the end-all, be-all, because he was so good at manipulating energy and matter. But, as he so poignantly pointed out (and these aren't his exact words), "You too are da' man."

I'm a single mom, not exactly the best "stereotype" in which to be cast. Like being black or Jewish, it brings up certain preconceived notions. People automatically expect me to be poor, maybe on welfare.

While that's certainly one of the available channels, I prefer to watch a different channel. I prefer to focus on a different reality.

Here's what it says on my website: Pam Grout is a world traveler, a loving mother, a best-selling author, a millionaire, and an inspiring witness to everyone she meets. I started focusing on those things 15 years ago before I'd ever had a child, before I became a travel writer, or an author and, for that matter, before I even liked myself all that much. Focusing on what I wanted obviously worked, because now I can proudly say all but one of the above are true. I'll let you guess which one is yet to manifest.

So far, I've written 13 books, two screenplays, a live soap opera, and enough magazine articles that I haven't starved in 14 years without a nine-to-five job. I write a travel column called, "Now, Where Was I?" that has taken me to all seven continents. I've written about everything from bungy jumping in New Zealand to carpet buying in Morocco to picking coffee in Nicaragua.

I'm also a reporter for *People* magazine. Working out of the Chicago Bureau, I've written about everything from a dinosaur hunter to a couple guys who opened a bakery for dogs.

I have yet to jump out of an airplane, but I have to save something for my 90th birthday.

ANECDOTAL EVIDENCE

"A ship in port is safe, but that is not what ships are built for."
—Benizar Bhutto, former prime minister of Pakistan

When he was 34, Augusten Burroughs decided to stop being an alcoholic and become a *New York Times* best-selling author. As he says in his most recent memoir, *Magical Thinking*, "The gap between active alcoholic copy writer living in squalor and literary sensation with a scrapbook of rave reviews seemed large. A virtual canyon. Yet one day, I decided that's exactly what I would do."

Fourteen days later, he finished his first manuscript, a novel called *Sellevision*.

"I did not expect it to be a bestseller. It was the cheese popcorn book. What I did expect was that it would be published," he says.

It was. And then he wrote a memoir about his childhood.

"And this, I decided, needed to be a *New York Times* bestseller, high on the list. It needed to be translated into a dozen languages and optioned for film," he writes.

His agent suggested he tone down his ambitions.

"I understood his point of view," Augusten says. "I also understood that the book would be huge—not because it was exceptionally well-written—but because it had to be so I could quit my loathsome advertising job and write full-time."

Augusten's memoir, *Running with Scissors*, spent over 70 consecutive weeks on the *New York Times* bestseller list. At last count, it has been published in over 15 countries. A film based on the book is currently in production.

"Luck? The greedy wishes of a desperate man randomly filled?" says Augusten. "No. There are no accidents."

THE METHOD:

"We are powerfully imprisoned by the terms in which we have been conducted to think."
—Buckminster Fuller

In this experiment, using nothing but the power of your thoughts, you will magnetize something into your life. You will set an intention to draw a particular event or thing into your life. Be specific. Down to the exact make and model.

Since you've only got 48-hours, it's probably best to pick something that won't drive your thoughts back to New Orleans. For example, if you decide to manifest a BMW Z3 2.8

Roadster, it's quite possible your predominant thoughts will be "Yeah right, eat my shorts." Needless to say, thoughts like that won't take you all the way to Biloxi. Not that you couldn't manifest a BMW Z3 Roadster (there are gurus in India who pluck jewels from thin air), but, for the sake of paradigm shifting, let's start with baby steps. Pick something you can get your mind around. Like a front row theater ticket. Or a phone call from a long lost lover.

Chuck, for example, decided to be a wiseass. He wanted to sleep with two girls at one time. Sure enough, by the end of his 48-hours, he met a new woman (who he now dates) and ended up in bed with her and her six-year-old daughter who crawled in for a quick snuggle with mom.

LAB REPORT SHEET

The Principle:
The Abracadabra Principle

The Theory:
Thoughts held in mind create after their kind.

The Question:
Can I pull things out of thin air simply by thinking about them?

The Hypothesis:
By making the following intention and focusing on its outcome, I can draw it into my life.

The Intention:
Within 48 hours, I want to magnetize _____ into my life.

Time required:
48 hours

Today's Date:

Time:

Deadline for manifesting:

Research Notes:

Research Notes Continued:

_____

_____

_____

_____

_____

_____

_____

_____

_____

_____

_____

_____

_____

_____

_____

_____

_____

_____

_____

_____

_____

_____

THE DEAR ABBY PRINCIPLE

Cosmo's K's loving counsel is ongoing, immediate,
and available any time night or day.

"I have often wished that when struggling with a dilemma the clouds would part, and a cosmic Charlton Heston-type voice would invite us to the second floor, where the Librarian of Life would sit with us for several hours, patiently answering all questions, and giving direction."
—Henriette Anne Klauser

PREMISE:

There's never a time—never has been, never will be—when you can't call on Cosmo K for assistance. For anything.

Relying on any other decision-making tool is asking for trouble. The conscious mind—where all the rattle, buzz-buzz, what-do-I-do-what-do-I-do? goes on—was never designed to solve problems. It's like using a pair of fingernail clippers to cut the lawn. Yet, that's where all of us get our guidance—from a left cerebral hemisphere that's prone to misjudgment, faulty interpretations, and major fabrications.

The conscious mind was designed for just two things—to identify problems and formulate goals.

Anyone using the mind properly would use it to define a problem or to set an intention and then jump back, Jack. That's it. That's all the cerebral cortex is good for. But instead, the conscious mind decides to get involved, to weigh the pros and cons, to come to "rational decisions," gut feelings be damned.

No sooner does the conscious mind define the problem or set the intention than it begins the yammer. It yammers on and on about how big the problem is and why it's not likely to get solved anytime soon and how that intention sounds cool, but geez, I've been there, done that, and it sure as heck didn't pan out last time. Suffice it to say, this spin doctor in the brain is not your best resource. It judges, distorts, and causes unnecessary emotional distress.

Let's take a quick look at how it works. Say Judy uses her conscious mind to create the intention of improving her relationship with her husband. Perfect! Great job! Except that instead of pulling back and letting the intention flower, instead of temporarily shelving the conscious mind and turning to a source that could really offer some assistance, Judy's conscious mind begins creating "rational" conclusions, begins considering options. Before long, it's screaming, "Don't get me started."

And from there it begins to sound like a band of rock star wanna-be's jamming in their parent's garage:

"My relationship with my husband is a charade."

"My husband is needy and lazy."

"I'll never get what I want."

In other words, the conscious mind starts interpreting. The problem is it can't even speak English. The results can be messy, capricious, and cruel.

A better tact is to use those fingernail clippers for what they're designed for, put them back in the medicine cabinet, and get out a tool that's better equipped for mowing the lawn—inner guidance.

Once you get the hang of it, you'll find it's extremely reliable. Plus, its answers are far more peaceful, instinctive, and responsive to all the unpredictable factors that the conscious mind can't begin to understand.

INNER GUIDANCE COMES IN MANY PACKAGES

"I have no idea what the source of my inner voice is. I certainly do not believe it is the voice of Jesus Christ, or a dead ancestor with a quavery Irish brogue, or a high-ranking Plediadian sending me physic data packets from a spaceship—although that last notion would be especially fun."

—D. Patrick Miller

Sometimes inner guidance comes completely unbidden. Like the night I was fretting about my newborn daughter's 106-degree temperature. I was pacing the floor with Tasman in my arms, frantic with worry, and completely baffled as to how to bring the raging fever under control. It was around 3 AM, and while my friends always say "Call me anytime night or day" and probably even mean it, I couldn't bring myself to do it. Instead, I walked back and forth across our little apartment, crying out in complete despair at the funeral I feared I'd soon be planning. Suddenly, a voice of startling clarity surfaced in my mind. It said, "I didn't give you this great gift just to take it away."

Sometimes inner guidance offers messages as distinct as those eight-ball fortune-telling toys. Darlene had what at-the-time seemed like a rather foolish vision. She felt guided to apply for a music director position at her church in North Carolina. Sounded good except for one small detail—she had absolutely no musical training and could only play the alto sax ... badly. Sure, she loved to sing, but loving to sing and getting a team of musicians to play instruments and singers to create harmony are two different balls of wax. Her conscious mind started its spin doctoring. "Darlene, you are just plum nuts. Why would God . . . or anyone else . . . want you to lead a music team?"

So she agreed to give it one last shot—a shot from half-court, no less—after which time she reassured herself she'd file the vision where it probably belonged—in the local garbage dumpster.

She made the following bargain with God. If you really want me to lead the music team, have me run into either the minister, the board president, or the pianist by the end of today. Since it was Monday and church was already sealed and delivered for that week, she figured she was safe. After all, she worked all day and the odds of running into one of those three characters in her neighborhood were next to zilcho.

On the way home from work, she remembered that she needed to stop at Sam's Club for a couple groceries. She walks up to the check out line when she hears a voice. "Yoo-hoo, Darlene. What are you doing here?"

It wasn't an ethereal voice from the deep like the reassuring voice that comforted me at 3 AM. It was the voice of Mary Jenkins, board president, who was waiting in line for a printer ink cartridge.

The point is guidance comes in all packages. For many years, just before he went to sleep, Napoleon Hill, author of the classic *Think and Grow Rich*, would call an imaginary council meeting of Ralph Waldo Emerson, Thomas Paine, Thomas Edison, Charles Darwin, Abraham Lincoln, Luther Burbank, Henry Ford, Napoleon, and Andrew Carnegie. As chairman of this imaginary cabinet, Hill was able to ask questions and get advice.

THE DEAR ABBY PRINCIPLE

After some months of these night-time proceedings, Hill was astounded that the appointees on his cabinet developed individual characteristics. Lincoln, for example, developed the habit of coming late, then walking around in solemn parade. Burbank and Paine often engaged in witty repartee.

"These experiences were so canny, so realistic that I became fearful of their consequences and finally quit," Hill admitted.

Like many people who receive unusual inner guidance, Hill was reticent to admit to his nightly council meetings.

But he did say this. "While the members of my cabinet may be purely fictional, they have led me into glorious paths of adventure, rekindled an appreciation of true greatness, encouraged creative endeavor, and emboldened the expression of honest thought."

Inner guidance can come in any package you're open enough to hear. Some of us need a big whack on the side of the head. Others, like Gary Renard, author of *The Disappearance of the Universe*, who has an extremely open mind, got guidance from a couple ascended masters who showed up one night while he was watching TV.

Michael Beckwith, before he became a powerful New Thought minister at the Agape Church of Love in Los Angeles, saw a vision of a scroll unrolled that read, "Michael Beckwith to speak at the Tacoma Church of Religious Science." When the Tacoma pastor called, he said, "Hey, Michael, we'd like you to come speak at our church."

Michael said, "I know."

WHY GUIDANCE SOMETIMES SEEMS LIKE THE EASTER BUNNY

"No matter how much evidence you have, over time you tend to block out experiences that aren't 'normal.'"

—Martha Beck

Unfortunately, most of us have restricted the guidance we'll let in. We've decided that neon, telegrams, and sealed letters from God are okay, but everything else is well, just a bit too frightening.

Hell, we'd be scared witless if a scroll unrolled in front of us or an ascended master stepped in front of a rerun of *Friends*. Our neural pathways have said, "Uh, uh, not me, I'm not up for that." If some angel showed up at the foot of our bed, we'd probably call the police.

It has to be challenging. How would you feel if someone asked you a question and then turned their back and ignored everything you said? We're like five-year-olds with our fingers in our ears going, "La-la-la-la-la."

You wouldn't just pick up your phone when it rings and start talking loudly. You'd say "hello" and listen to the person on the other end of the line.

Here we are accusing the God force of not giving us clear guidance and we're the ones with our damned phones off the hook.

When Neale Donald Walsh first sat down with a pen in his hand and some tough questions in his heart, he was shell-shocked when the God force answered, "Do you really want to know the answer? Or are you just ranting?" Walsh, who somewhat hesitantly agreed to play along, says, "Well, both. But if you've got answers, I'd love to hear them."

Religious types, of course, cried "blasphemy, heresy." Who does he think he is, speaking directly to God?

Well, hello, who wouldn't want to talk to the source of everything?

They believe Jesus talked with God and the Jewish prophets talked with God, but that was, that was . . . .

Yes, I'm waiting.

WE PUT GOD ON THE NO-CALL LIST.

"One of the main functions of formalized religions is to protect people against a direct experience of God."
—Carl Jung

Where did we ever pick up the foolhardy notion that God would stop communicating with us? Even Ann Landers kept giving advice, writing that column right up to her death from cancer in 2002.

A lot of it goes back to those myths we believe about God. That's he's oh-so mysterious and only on-call Sundays. The part that was left out is that God's direction is reliable and constantly available. It's there any time you choose to listen, same as CNN is on anytime you decide to switch on the TV. It's that reliable.

And you are free to put it on the spot, to demand clear answers. Now.

Michael Beckwith, the guy I mentioned earlier who got the scroll, was looking up at a windmill one day. This is before he became a minister and wasn't completely convinced that his decision to pursue God was the right one. He says to God, point blank, "Look God, if you're listening, if this is what you really want for me, have that windmill point in my direction."

Even though it was a windy day and the windmill was spinning to beat the band in the other direction, no sooner did he say that than that windmill stopped rotating at its normal axis and pointed straight at him.

Sometimes, the God force even manages to get through to people who scoff at it. In 1975, Gerald Jampolsky, a successful California psychiatrist on the outside, was falling apart on the inside. His 20-year-marriage had ended. He was drinking heavily. He developed chronic, disabling back pain. Of course, it never dawned on him to seek higher guidance.

As he says, "I was the last person to be interested in a thought system that used words like God and love."

But nonetheless, when he first saw the Course in Miracles, a book that teaches personal transformation by choosing love rather than fear, he heard a voice clearly tell him, "Physician, heal thyself. This is your way home."

And, of course, it was. Jampolsky has gone on to write many books, he lectures widely on the principles of the Course in Miracles, and he even started a center in Sausalito for people with life-threatening illnesses.

Immediate, direct guidance is available 24/7. But instead of paying attention, we taught ourselves the most unnatural habit of not communicating with Cosmo K. It's like the foreign exchange student from Myanmar who didn't grow up around technology and has no idea that the phone beside his bed could hook him up with that cute girl in his biology class. He thinks he has to wait until tomorrow to talk to her.

ANECDOTAL EVIDENCE:

"If only God would give me a clear sign. Like making a large deposit in my name at a Swiss bank."
—Woody Allen

Twenty years ago, when she was 25, Jamie Lee Curtis was hanging out in her recently-purchased Los Angeles apartment with her friend, Debra Hill. Debra, who had produced *Halloween*, the spooky movie that launched Jamie Lee's career, had brought over the current issue of *Rolling Stone* as a housewarming gift. They were flipping through the magazine and chatting optimistically about the end of Jamie Lee's most recent relationship, when they turned to a photograph of three men.

Jamie Lee pointed to the man on the right, who was wearing a plaid shirt and a waggish smirk, and told Debra, "I'm going to marry that man."

She'd never seen him before, had no idea who he was, but something inside told her he was "the one."

"That's Christopher Guest," Debra said. "He's in a funny new movie called *This is Spinal*

Tap. I know his agent."

Jamie Lee, awestruck by this very clear churning in her gut, called the agent the next day, gave him her number, and told him to have Chris call her if he was interested.

He never called.

Several months later, while at Hugo's, a popular West Hollywood restaurant, Jamie Lee glanced up to find herself staring straight at the guy from the magazine, only three tables away. He waved as if to say, "I'm the guy you called." She waved back.

"Hmm," she's thinking, "Interesting." Except a few minutes later, he gets up to leave. He shrugs, waves, and walks out the door. Jamie looks down at her plate, kicking herself for believing in something as stupid as "inner guidance."

But the next day, her phone rings. It's Chris Guest and he wants to set up a date. Four days later, at Chianti Ristorante on Melrose, they met for dinner and a month and a few days later, when he left for New York to tape a year of *Saturday Night Live*, they'd fallen head over heels in love.

Jamie Lee Curtis and Christopher Guest were married December 18, 1984, eight months after she got that initial guidance. They recently celebrated 20 years of wedded bliss.

THE METHOD:

"Parting the Red Sea, and turning water to blood, the burning bush...nothing like that was going on now. Not even in New York City."
—Michael Crichton

In this experiment, we'll prove that the guidance received by Jamie Lee Curtis is not some weird, *Twilight Zone* anomaly, but a very real and ongoing tool that all of us can use at any time.

We'll spend 48 hours expecting a specific, concrete answer to a specific, concrete question. It can be as simple as whether to get a new Siamese kitten neutered or as complicated as whether or not to take a job offer. We give God 48 hours to spell it out. But watch out. One time I tried this and got fired. In retrospect, it was the perfect answer, maybe the only one I could hear, to the question I'd asked, "Is it time to launch my freelance writing career?"

Choose an issue that is troubling you, something that has a yes or no answer, something on which you're really confused and don't know what to do. I know you're thinking of something right now, doesn't matter what it is. That issue will work. Look at your watch.

Forty-eight hours from now, ask for a clear-non-debatable sign.

For example, when I was writing this book, I wanted to come up with a different name for the God force. Like I said, the word God is laden with more baggage than your average moving van and I thought it would be helpful to start with a whole new concept.

Here's what I said. By 2 o'clock Friday (2:24 on my computer), my intention is to have a compelling new name for the God force. Well, sure enough, by 2 pm Cosmo K came to me, along with a whole plan for selling buttons that say, "I believe in Cosmo K."

It's your job to set the intention and the time frame. The force will do the rest.

Stan (remember the cute former surfer from Esalen?) had lost his job. To make matters worse, his girlfriend of three years decided it was time to move on. Needless to say, he had some pretty serious decisions to make. First on the old agenda, Stan decided, was to find a way to make some money. But he had no idea what he wanted to do. I reminded him there was a Divine Plan for his life and that it would be revealed if he simply set the intention and a deadline, like say, next Friday morning.

Stan said something like this, "Hey, dude, if it's true that you have a plan for my life, I could use a directional pointer. I don't have a lot of time, so by Friday morning, I want to know just what you have in mind for me."

On Thursday afternoon, Stan was sitting in the hot springs with a man he'd never met. The man happened to mention he was opening a self-improvement center out in the Laurel Highlands of Pennsylvania and was looking for someone to run the place. Stan immediately felt a buzz and, sure enough, not 30 minutes later, was offered the job even though the sum total of his job experience at a self-improvement center was cabin cleaner.

Chalk one up for the Dude!

LAB REPORT SHEET

The Principle:
The Dear Abby Principle

The Theory:
Cosmo's K's loving counsel is ongoing, immediate, and available any time night or day.

The Question:
Is it really possible to get ongoing, immediate guidance?

The Hypothesis.
If I ask Cosmo K for clear guidance on a specific yes or no question, I will get a clear answer to the following yes or no question:

The Question:

Time required:
48 hours

Today's Date:

Time:

Deadline for receiving answer:

The Approach:
Say something like this: Okay God, I need to know the answer to this question. You've got 48 hours. Make it snappy.

Research Notes:

THE SALLY FIELD PRINCIPLE

**The Dude Likes You. He
Really Likes You.**

"The truth dazzles gradually, or else the world would be blind."
—Emily Dickinson

PREMISE:

Most of us equate God with Triple A. Good to call when you break down. What this principle states is that contrary to popular opinion, the dude is actually quite fond of you and wants nothing more than to rain down blessings upon your head.

Bottom line is you have no conception of the limits you have placed on your perception.

Your confusion is so profound that you cannot even conceive of the world without sacrifice. But here's the thing: the world contains no sacrifice except what you laid upon it.

It's worth pausing for a moment to consider just how deluded we've become.

A few days after Eckhart Tolle's 29th birthday, he was suffering an intense, suicidal anxiety attack. His life so far had basically sucked sewer slime. On this particular night, he kept saying to himself, over and over again, "I cannot live with myself any longer." Suddenly, he says, "I could feel myself being sucked into a void."

When he "woke up," all he could experience was love, a state of deep, uninterrupted peace and bliss.

His intense pain forced his consciousness to withdraw from all the limits he had placed on it. The withdrawal was so complete that his deluded self, his unhappy and deeply fearful self, immediately collapsed like an inflatable toy without a plug.

He spent almost two years doing nothing but sitting on park benches in a state of intense joy.

"Okay," you're thinking. "I'm starting to feel uncomfortable now." Or you're flat-out bamboozled, wondering how in the hell did he support himself? How did he eat?

Thoughts like those simply point out that you're still playing by the world's delusions.

Or consider Byron Katie. This California realtor was in the middle of an ordinary life—two marriages, three kids, a successful career—when she went into a deep depression. She checked herself into a halfway house for women with eating disorders, not because she had an eating disorder but because it was the only facility her insurance company would cover. One night, while lying on the floor in the attic ("I didn't feel worthy enough to sleep in a bed," she says), she suddenly woke up without any of life's normal preconceived notions of sacrifice.

"Everything was unrecognizable. All thoughts that had troubled me, my whole world was gone. Laughter welled up from the depths and just poured out. I was intoxicated with joy," she says.

Like Tolle, she went home and sat by the window, staring out in complete bliss for days on end.

"It was like freedom had woken up inside me," she says.

COLONEL MUSTARD IN THE CONSERVATORY WITH THE WRENCH

"Common sense is the collection of prejudices acquired by age eighteen."
—Albert Einstein

I was playing the board game *Clue* with a couple of my daughter's friends. We passed out the detective notebooks and placed the rope, the lead pipe, and the other miniature weapons in the miniature mansion's miniature rooms.

I said to Kylie, who because she was sitting closest to the purple token was playing Professor Plum, "Why don't you go first?"

The two girls looked at me as if I'd just asked them to take a shower in the boy's locker room.

"Mom, Miss Grout!" they loudly protested.

"What? What did I say?"

"Everybody knows Miss Scarlett always goes first."

Likewise, they explained that in order to make an accusation you have to be in the room where you think the murder took place and if you want to take a secret passageway, you can only do it between the parlor and the kitchen or the library and the conservatory.

"Who says?" I asked.

"The rules. It says so right here." One of them thrust the neatly-printed rule sheet in my face.

These 'engraved-in-stone' rules remind me of how we play "life." Somebody—they say, I guess—decided that this is how the world works, and because we all agreed to "see it that way," we made it a "reality."

Turns out, we've all been had. Nearly all the concepts and judgments we take for granted are gross distortions of things as they really are. Everything we think is "real" is simply a reflection of the "Clue rules" we all agreed upon. The world we think we see is merely the projection of our own individual "Clue rules."

Maybe it's time to take those Clue rules, cut them up, and use them as confetti. Until we do, until we finally get it that we are "wholly loved, wholly loveable, and wholly loving," we will continue to feel empty, question our purpose, and wonder why we're here.

That's why we need to ask for a whole new lens for looking at the world. We need to know he likes us, he really likes us.

ANECDOTAL EVIDENCE:

"Being gloomy is easier than being cheerful. Anybody can say 'I've got cancer' and get a rise out of a crowd. But how many of us can do five minutes of good stand-up comedy?"
—P.J. O'Rourke

For years, Myrtle Fillmore's life revolved around her cabinet full of medicine. Not only did she suffer from tuberculosis that caused her to spit up blood and run a near-constant fever, but she also had aggravated malaria. One day, she attended a lecture by a New Thought teacher who made the outrageous claim that God, who was all-good, would never wish disease on anyone. Furthermore, this Dr. Weeks said, that if she aligned herself with this all-good spirit, she would discover her true self—which was healthy.

Over and over, Myrtle began affirming, "I am a child of God and therefore I do not inherit sickness." She refused to "judge according to appearance" and praised the vital energy of God within every cell of her body. Little by little, Myrtle began to get better. Within two years, there was no sign of any of her old illnesses.

Myrtle's husband, Charles, witnessed the remarkable healing of his wife and decided to try the same affirmations. He, too, was considered disabled. Thanks to a skating accident he'd had as a boy and a series of operations, his hip socket was badly damaged and one of his legs had stopped growing. He wore a steel extension to make his legs even. He just figured the best he could do was learn to live with the chronic pain.

Like Myrtle, Charles Fillmore began to affirm an all-good, all-powerful energy force. Not only was he completely cured of pain within a year, but his shortened leg caught up with the other one.

THE METHOD:

"Reality is only an illusion, albeit, a persistent one."
—Albert Einstein

This experiment will prove what Sally Field finally figured out when she won the Oscar for *Norma Rae.* "You like me, you really like me." It will prove how sublime our world truly is.

For the next 48 hours, we're going to keep track of goodness and beauty.

The record of history, of course, is written in blood—in wars, treachery, and competition. But as paleontologist Stephen Jay Gould says, "The fossil record shows long, uninterrupted periods of biological stability."

Gould says it's a structural paradox that one violent act so distracts us from the 10,000 acts of kindness. Human courtesy, kindness, and beauty, he says, are the norm.

He calls it our duty, our holy responsibility to record and honor the victorious weight of all the innumerable little kindnesses that are all too often unnoted and invisible.

Here are some examples of what you might tick off:

1. My wife gave me a kiss before I left for my doctor's appointment.
2. The receptionist and I compared pictures of her new baby and my new grandson.
3. When I entered my office with an armload of books, a stranger held the door for me.
4. The man at the lunch counter smiled and said, "Wassup?"
5. Students in the overcrowded lunchroom graciously shared a table.
6. My e-mail misbehaved, and a colleague helped me sort it out.
7. A colleague in another state responded to my testy message with grace and good will.

LAB REPORT SHEET

The Principle:
The Sally Field Principle

The Theory:
The dude likes you. He really likes you.

The Question:
Is my focus on the negative keeping me from seeing reality?

The Hypothesis:
If I make a concerted effort to look for goodness beauty, it will show up in spades.

Time required:
48 hours

Today's Date:

Time:

Number of kind, beautiful, good things:

The Approach:
Say this or something like it. As you probably know, God, you've had this major PR glitch. Somebody's been spreading the rumor that you're a judgmental, rule-making wise ass. Course, I've also heard that you love me and want nothing but my happiness. So which is it?

I hate to be greedy here, but I need to know.

I'm ready to put my faith in you. I'm tired of working so hard, plum sick of knocking myself out to get ahead. I'd love nothing more than to step aside and let you take over.

Research Notes:

GODLETS R US

You are not bound by the laws of this world.

"Ray, when someone asks if you're god, you say yes!"
—Winston Zeddmore to Dan Aykroyd in *Ghostbusters*

MATTER DOES NOT CONTROL YOU. YOU CONTROL MATTER.

"The course of the world is not predetermined by physical laws . . . the mind has the power to affect groups of atoms and even tamper with the odds of atomic behavior."
—Sir Arthur Stanley Eddington, English mathematician and astrophysicist

Masaru Emoto, a Japanese scientist, spent 15 years researching the effects of human's speech, thoughts, and emotions on physical matter. Dr. Emoto chose one of matter's four elements—water—to see how it responds to words, music, prayers, and blessings. Using more than 10,000 samples of water, Emoto and his research assistants spoke to water, played music to water, showed movies to water, and asked monks to recite prayers to water. The samples were then frozen and the resulting ice crystals examined under a microscope.

In case you're wondering what water has to do with anything, dig this. Water is present everywhere—even in the air—and since the human body and indeed the earth consists of 70 percent water, it stands to reason that if words and thoughts impact water, they will also affect larger, more complex systems also made up of water.

What Emoto found is that when scientists treated the water "kindly," by saying such things as "thank you" and "I love you," the resulting water crystals were clear and beautifully-formed. When Emoto and his team dissed the water, screamed such snide comments as "I hate you" or "you idiot," the crystals formed dark, ugly holes. When Elvis Presley's

"Heartbreak Hotel" was played to water, the resulting frozen crystal split in two.

In one photo, he shows how a sample from the dam at Fujiwara lake, starting out as a dark and amorphous blob, is completely transformed after a priest prays over it for just one hour. The ugly crystal turned into a clear, bright-white hexagonal crystal-within-a-crystal. He also found that prayer could create new types of crystals, never before seen.

SICKNESS IS OPTIONAL

"Things not always what seem."
—Kesuke Miyagi in *The Karate Kid*

I should probably have my head examined for including this section in the book. You'll notice I've hidden it in the middle of a long chapter near the back.

It's not that you haven't heard ideas like this before—that so and so's cancer was caused by unresolved anger or that stress can turn hair white overnight. But what I'm going so far as to say is that we've been led down the garden path by a bloated, greedy medical system that has convinced us disease is inevitable. I am not knocking doctors, nurses, or other medical personnel, 99.9 percent of whom are caring, committed, and well-meaning. No, they're just as hoodwinked as we are. What I'm suggesting is that the erroneous consciousness of all of us has resulted in major computer errors. Instead of seeing sickness as a problem, something to correct, we accept it as a fact of life. We've all agreed to this arbitrary set of rules that says sickness can't be escaped, that illness is natural. Most of us can't even imagine perfect health.

Long ago, our minds established this false pattern of perception. Once a mind thinks it can't do some task (like unclog an artery), it informs the brain that it can't do it, which in turn informs the muscles. The virus in our consciousness has limited our ability to utilize our bodies' great wisdom.

But our belief in the inevitability of a degenerating body only *seems* real because we've believed it to be real for so long. Dr. Alex Carrel, a French physician, won the Nobel prize in medicine for demonstrating that cells can be kept alive indefinitely. His research proved "there's no reason cells need to degenerate. Ever."

"The education we all get is that we have no power, that we don't know anything," says Meir Scheider, a man who cured himself of blindness, "but it's not true. Within each of us is everything we need to know."

When Meir was born in Lvov, Ukraine in 1954, he was cross-eyed, had glaucoma, astigmatism, mystagmus, and several other hard-to-pronounce diseases. His cataracts were so severe that he was forced to endure six major surgeries before he turned seven. The last one broke the lens on his eyeball and by the time he was in second grade, he was declared legally blind. So much for modern medicine.

When Meir was 17, he met a kid named Isaac who had a different message than the doctors and surgeons. Isaac, who was all of 16, actually had the gall to tell him, "If you want, you can train yourself to see."

No one had ever had that kind of faith before. All he'd ever heard was, "you poor, poor blind thing."

Meir's family, like any good, sympathetic family, discouraged him from getting his hopes up. Sure, try the exercises, they said, but don't forget—you're a blind kid. Within a year, as Isaac predicted, Meir began to see . . . not a lot at first, but enough to believe that maybe this 16-year-old kid knew more than the doctors who wrote him off as blind and inoperable.

Eventually, Schneider gained enough vision to read, to walk, to run, and to drive. Today, he's the proud owner of a California driver's license where he lives and operates a self-healing center.

"Blind people," he says, "become more blind because they aren't expected to see. They're thrown into a category."

Furthermore, he can't understand why an optimistic concept sounds so bizarre to most people.

When Barbra Streisand was a young girl growing up in Brooklyn, she fell in love with the movies. She wanted nothing more than to be a glamorous movie star. Unfortunately, her widowed mother was dirt poor and she wasn't exactly Grace Kelly material. Any reasonable career counselor would have encouraged her to pursue a different goal. "After all, honey, you have an unconventional nose and, well, how can I put this politely? You being an actress is like Kareem Abdul Jabbar wanting to be a jockey."

But Barbra's intentions were SO strong that I believe she manipulated matter through the only pathway she could—a voice so powerful that led to stardom on Broadway and eventually into the movies.

SPEAKING OF FAMILIES . . .

"My mind is a bad neighborhood I try not to go into alone."
—Anne Lamott

When I was born on February 17, 1956, my father took one look at me, laying there helplessly in my pink basinette, and announced to my mother that I was the ugliest baby he had ever seen. Needless to say, my mother was devastated. And I, a minutes-old human being, decided right then and there that beauty—or lack thereof—was destined to color every moment of my life.

My Dad's life-changing indictment was prompted by my nose which was plastered to my face like a roadkill possum. After 18-hours of grueling labor, the obstetrician decided to intervene with a pair of cold, metal forceps. In the battle between the forceps and me, my nose got flattened.

Gradually, the nose bounced back to normal, but my fragile ego remained disfigured. I desperately wanted to be beautiful. I wanted to prove to my father that I was acceptable and to make up to my mother for the embarrassment I caused her.

I scoured beauty magazines, studying the models like a biologist studying cells. I rolled my hair with orange juice cans and ordered green face masks and blackhead pumps from the back of *Seventeen* magazine. I saved my allowance to buy a set of Clairol electric rollers. I wore gloves to bed to keep the hand-softening vaseline from staining the sheets. I even clipped "interesting" hair styles from the Montgomery Ward catalog, pasteing them to the back page of my own personal "beauty book."

This personal beauty book, besides the 50 heads with different hairstyles, listed my beauty goals: reduce my waist by five inches, increase my bust size by six inches, grow my hair, etc. And then, I included a page with plans for accomplishing each goal. To reduce my waist, for example, I would do 50 sit-ups each day, limit my morning pancake consumption to two, and give up Milky Way bars.

Despite my well-meaning attempts, I remained less than beautiful. No matter what I did, I never could seem to get my looks together. How could I? My very existence centered around my Dad's "ugly baby" statement. It was the first sentence of my life, the proclamation around which my very life revolved. To go against it would be dishonoring everything I knew—my Dad, my Mom, myself.

Things went from bad to worse. By sixth grade, my eyesight gave out and I was forced to wear a pair of black horn-rimmed glasses. By ninth grade, when I finally convinced Dad to invest in contacts, a definite beauty booster, my face immediately broke out in a dot-to-dot puzzle of pimples. All my babysitting money went for Clearasil, astringent, and Angelface makeup. One summer, after I heard zits were caused by chocolates and soft drinks, I even gave up Coca-Cola and candy bars.

And if that wasn't bad enough, my sister, who had the good fortune to escape both the forceps and the ugliness indictment, pointed out that my front teeth were crooked. Once again, I campaigned for family funds to install braces.

The sad thing about all this work and effort is I had no idea that until I changed the deep-seated thoughts about myself that I'd remain "ugly." I could have exercised, applied makeup, and rolled my hair until eternity, but as long as my Dad's indictment was the virus on which I operated, I was destined to "be the ugliest baby he'd ever seen." Oh sure, I made temporary progress. I'd clear up my complexion or grow my hair or straighten my teeth, but before long, something else would happen to resume the old familiar "ugliness."

You see, my body had no choice but to follow the blueprints my thoughts had given it.

About this time, I discovered self-help books. It was an inevitable meeting. Any teenager who thinks she closely resembles Frankenstein needs all the self-esteem boosting she can find.

I started with *Your Erroneous Zones* by Dr. Wayne Dyer. I read Barbara Walter's book on how to make conversation. I learned how to win friends and influence people, how to power myself with positive thinking, and how to think and grow rich. All the reading eventually started to change the way I felt about myself. I actually started finding things I liked.

Even things about my looks. I was tall, for one thing, which meant I could more or less eat anything I wanted. And my thick hair was an asset. And my best friend's mother said I had perfectly-shaped eyebrows. Instead of looking for things I disliked, I started concentrating on things I liked. Like magic, my looks started improving. As I gave up the limiting thoughts about myself, the better I looked. The less I chastised that poor little ogre in the mirror, the more she started to change. The less I TRIED to change myself, the more I changed.

Miraculously, my eyesight returned to normal. I was finally able to throw away the pop bottle glasses . . . and the contacts. The complexion from hell cleared up and my teeth, after months of a retainer, began to match the teeth of my family. In fact, the only time I felt grotesquely ugly was when I'd visit my Dad and his second wife.

Although I didn't realize it at the time, I was changing my "looks" during those visits to satisfy my Dad's belief about me—or rather what I thought were his beliefs about me. I now know my Dad's remark was simply an off-handed comment. He meant no harm.

But I didn't know it at the time. I took his ugly baby comment to heart and acted it out in rich, vivid detail.

Even the poor eyesight, which some might argue is a genetic propensity, was solely my creation. Nobody else in my family (there were five of us) ever wore glasses. They all had 20/20 vision. Likewise, nobody else in my family wore braces. They all had picture perfect teeth.

"We would rather be ruined than changed. We would rather die in our dread than climb the cross of the moment and let our illusions die."
—W. H. Auden

When Terry McBride was 22, he ruptured a disk in his back working construction. After a year of chiropractic, osteopathy, and muscle relaxers, he decided to take the suggestion of an orthopedic surgeon who thought he should have his spine fused.

"I was told I'd be in the hospital a couple weeks, home for a couple weeks, in a brace for six months, and then good as new," McBride says.

Two days after the surgery, he came down with a dangerously high fever. He was rushed back to the hospital where doctors discovered that somehow during the surgery he had contracted the E Coli bacteria. During the next year, he had eight surgical procedures trying to get rid of the spreading infection. By the fifth surgery, he was transferred to the teaching hospital at University of Washington where as he says, "I was a celebrity. I had the worst case of osteomyelitis they'd ever seen."

On the night before the tenth surgery, his team of doctors walked somberly in to his room. They'd finally gotten good x-rays, x-rays that showed the infection was no longer just in his spine. It had spread to his pelvis, his abdomen, and down both legs. To get rid of it, they said, they were going to have to cut him open from end to end. They said that by doing this procedure, they could virtually guarantee they'd get rid of the infection. But they could also guarantee that he'd lose the use of his right leg.

"Terry," the doctor said, "If this infection is as bad as we think it is, you could also lose your left foot, control of your bowels and bladder, and there's a good chance you'll end up sexually impotent."

"Quite honestly," McBride says. "That's where they made their mistake."

"Now I don't know about you, but I showed up on this planet as a happy little boy who liked me," McBride says. "But it didn't take long to learn that the people in authority knew more about me than I did. I learned that I needed to pay attention and that it was the teachers who were going to tell me how good I was in school. The coaches were gonna tell me if I had any athletic ability. The music teacher would decide if I could sing. I learned early on to look outside myself for who I was."

"Now, I probably would have given them a leg," McBride continues. "But when those doctors started insisting that there was no possible way to come out of this surgery whole, I decided right then and there that no body was going to tell me who I was. I decided that very night that no longer was anyone with a fancy name badge going to determine my destiny."

It was the night that changed his life. McBride, who had been studying spiritual principles, announced to the whole room (the team of five doctors, his wife, and his two-year-old daughter) that there was a power in the universe and he was going to use it to make him whole and free.

When he first started saying such things, everybody said, "Right on, hold fast to your dreams." But after 10 surgeries, people began urging him to face reality, to quit focusing on his petty, ego-centered personal priorities.

"We're talking petty, ego-centered personal priorities such as having a body that was disease free, a back that was strong enough to pick up my daughter, petty, ego-centered priorities like going to the bathroom without a plastic bag," he says. "Some people started suggesting that maybe perfect health wasn't part of God's plan."

It all came to a head before the 18th surgery. By that time, McBride was 27 and madder than a pole cat: "Even as a good fundamentalist, I couldn't buy that I deserved 18 surgeries. Maybe I'd sinned enough for four or five, but not 18."

He was sent to talk to the hospital psychiatrist who sat him down and said, "Son, it's time to take off the rose-colored glasses. Now you think that to be a man, you've got to be able to stand on two legs, to fight in the war like your father did, but it's time to come work with me, to learn to accept that you're going to spend the rest of your life in a wheelchair."

He showed him his medical records that clearly stated: "Terry McBride's problems are not curable. He will have permanent disability and ongoing surgeries for the rest of his life."

"But I'm not my medical records," McBride insisted. "I'm not my past. There is a power in me. I live in a spiritual universe and spiritual law can set me free."

"Don't you think your body would have healed by now if it was going to be healed?" the psychiatrist said.

But McBride refused to give up. He went on to have 30 major surgeries over the course of 11 years, wore a colostomy bag. All the while he continued to affirm that health and wholeness was his spiritual destiny.

Finally, long after most of us would have given up, he walked out of the hospital a free and whole strapping young man. Today, he travels the country speaking about his journey, teaching people the truth about their divine magnificence.

As he says, "We are already free. The infinite power of God will back up our belief in sickness and want if that's what we choose. But we can also change our beliefs to health, love, joy, and peace. It's time to claim our oneness with God, to step boldly into our lives. You are God and this is the truth that will set you free."

THE METHOD:

"There are no limitations to the self except those you believe in."
—Seth

Since we don't have access to all of Masaru Emoto's microscopes and research assistants, we're going to affect matter by duplicating an experiment you might have tried back in grade school. Sprouting green bean seeds. Dr. Larry Dossey, in more than a half dozen books on prayer, has detailed fanatically-precise medical studies that have proven that intention on a particular physical outcome affects everything from rye seeds to women with breast cancer. Again, we're beginners, so we're going to start with green beans.

Equipment:

•Cardboard egg carton.

•Potting soil.

•Green bean seeds.

Instructions: Plant two beans in each of the 12 holes. Place them near a window. Water them every couple days. Make the following conscious intention: With my innate, divine energy, I will that the beans on the left side of the egg carton grow faster than the beans on the right.

Write down your observations for the next seven days.

In the meantime, you can experiment with something scientists call applied kinesiology. It may sound complicated, but it's really just an elementary method of testing how your body reacts to negative and positive statements, spoken aloud. Dr. John Goodheart pioneered applied kinesiology in the sixties when he discovered that muscles instantly became weak when the body was exposed to harmful substances and strong in the presence of anything therapeutic. In the next decade, Dr. John Diamond further discovered that muscles also respond to emotional and intellectual stimuli. Here's the simple version:

Touch the thumb and middle finger of each hand to form two rings. Now link them together. Pull the linked fingers of the right hand tightly against the left hand, exerting just enough pressure so they hold. Get a feel for how that feels.

Now say this:

"My name is (say your name.)"

At the same time, exert the same amount of pressure.

Since I'm assuming you're not telling a fib, this statement will probably show that your hand stays strong and steady.

GOD DOESN'T HAVE BAD HAIR DAYS

Now say: "My name is Julia Roberts."

If you exert the same amount of pressure as before, the fingers should break apart.

Try several true and false statements until you get the calibration down. If the circle holds, it indicates a positive response: if the fingers of the right hand were able to break the connection of your left hand, the answer is "no way."

Not only is this an effective tool for getting your body's advice, but it's useful for testing how your body responds to statements such as the following:

"I am a huge dorkball."

"I am loving, passionate, peaceful, and happy."

"I hate my body."

"I am strong and powerful."

LAB REPORT SHEET

The Principle:
Godlets R Us

The Theory:
You are not bound by laws of this world.

The Question:
Is it possible to affect physical matter with my attention?

The Hypothesis:
If I focus my attention on a row of green bean seeds, I can make them sprout faster.

Time required:
Seven days

Today's Date:

Time:

The Approach:
God, god, god. I don't mean to be uppity here, but, c'mon, are you really trying to tell me that I can turn water into wine? That I can walk on water? That I can actually do everything that Jesus did?

Research Notes:

THE HARRY HOUDINI PRINCIPLE

Everything that doesn't look like love is smoke and mirrors.

"It is all about love and how we all are connected."
—Mark Wahlberg

PREMISE:

In this experiment you'll learn the most carefully-guarded secret in the world. Ready?

This century's most effective cover-up is this: all of us humans really love each other. Deeply.

The problem is we've gone to great lengths to make the opposite perception appear true. We've erected a lot of smoke and mirrors to keep this little-known secret from getting out.

And it's worked.

But it doesn't make it true. Any more than David Copperfield really makes his assistants disappear.

Because the love secret is still under wraps in most hearts of the world, we've got wars and poverty and other disasters that appear—at first glance at least—not to be so loving. Which gives even more ammunition (literally) to the illusion. Again, whatever we focus on expands.

Anytime the love secret threatens to peek around the corner, a 27-inch box in the corner of most of our living rooms (and kitchen and bedrooms) makes sure "the preposterous rumor" gets sidelined immediately.

If you pay attention to the 27-inch box, and most of us pretty much use it to form our view of reality, you have little choice but to conclude that murder, rape, war, and genocide is the human condition. As humorist P.J. O'Rourke likes to say, "Violence is interesting which makes it a great obstacle to world peace and more thoughtful television programming."

But spiritual principle tells us otherwise. Love is the only thing that's real.

As it stands now on most channels of our reality, we see a mere fraction of our fellow humanoids. We see the outer picture—the frame, as it were. I liken it to going to the Louvre and, instead of looking at the Mona Lisa, spending three hours admiring the gold, gilt frame that surrounds her.

This might be okay except that by looking at your brother's weaknesses, that perception grows in yourself. As my mother used to say whenever I tried to poke fun at a classmate, "Any insult is incapable of leaving its source."

If, on the other hand, you practice viewing your brother as innocent and loving, those attributes grow within yourself.

To be blunt, our endless judgments have imprisoned us. They've kept us separate, they've made us fearful.

YEAH, BUT . . . .

"Squint your eyes and look closer . . ."
—Ani DiFranco

I know, I've seen the news, too. But if you look at it scientifically, the math just doesn't work out. For every Scott Peterson, there're 66.3 million fathers in America who didn't murder their wives.

People accuse me of being an irresponsible parent when they hear I haven't taught my daughter lesson number 82. You know the one: "It's dangerous to talk to strangers." But I refuse to impart that lesson because I don't want her thinking people are scary. They're not. People are really nice and generous and loving and there is only one thing that keeps us from seeing that—our fear.

Because those ubiquitous 27-inch boxes focus on tragedy and disaster, most of us have actually bought into this ridiculous notion that the world is a dangerous place and that people cannot be trusted.

The other Tuesday, the news media in Kansas City was all abuzz with "an important news story" about a two-year-old girl who had allegedly been abducted. It was breaking news on the six o'clock newscasts for all four local television stations.

It seems Jenna, the two-year-old, disappeared while her mother was vacuuming the carpets about 4:15 PM. Her brother, who was all of four-years-old, told mom that he thought Jenna had toddled out the back door without her clothes on. Frantic mom rushes outside and since Jenna isn't in the backyard or the front yard, immediately calls 911. Dozens of police officers show up, begin organizing detailed neighborhood searches. Television cameramen set up camp in the front yard. An Amber Alert is promptly declared.

Whatever "news" the TV channels had planned for that night got tossed aside while somber-looking anchors yammered on and on about the poor, unfortunate, and now missing two-year-old. Channel 5 devoted more than ten minutes of its 30-minute newscast to reiterating the same few details, showing her oh-so-darling picture every 30 seconds or so.

Channel 9 displayed the "Amber Alert" banner over its normal programming for at least the next half-hour after the news.

Of course, after 30 minutes, they couldn't do it with a straight face. You see, nobody ever thought to check the apartment. It seems little Jenna didn't like the sound of mom's vacuum cleaner, so she crawled inside a bedroom closet to take a nap.

Every day, it seems, our TV stations give us "news" about missing children, identity theft, the mild-mannered neighbor who walks into work one day with an AK-57 and blows up his boss and 27 co-workers.

Why do we think this is news?

The same day Karissa, a two-year-old from Kentucky who really was abducted from her home in Louisville (by her father, as it turns out), there were 53,298 two-year-olds in Kentucky who didn't get abducted, who were safe and sound at home, happily sipping apple juice from their Winnie-the-Pooh high chairs. Nearly a million children of all ages in Kentucky also didn't get abducted that same day.

Why is Karissa the "news"?

News, by definition, is new information that teaches people about the world. Picking out what happened to two-one thousandth of one percent of the state's two-year-olds is not an accurate picture of the world. If you ask me, what happened to the other 53,298 two-year-olds is a bigger story. Or at least it's more realistic news.

What you see on the newscasts at night, what you read in the morning newspaper is not a realistic perception of our world. It's an anomaly, an out-of-character thing that happened that one day in time. We must keep that in perspective.

News junkies pride themselves on believing they're well-informed. Because they know what Tom Brokaw said about the latest layoffs at Boeing and what Morley Safer reported on the flood in Indiana, they smugly believe they're up on current events. But do they know about the African-American postman in Germantown, Tennessee who jumped into a lake to save a couple whose brakes went out of their car when they were coming home from a hospital dialysis treatment? Do they know about the Marysville, Kansas attorney who flew, on his own dime, to Israel to donate a kidney to a 10-year-old he'd never met?

Thinking you're informed because you watch the news every night is like thinking you understand a zoo when you've only seen the "Z" on the entryway sign. It's not a complete picture, guys. It's not even a good picture. I'm not going to argue that you can't find the letter "Z" at any zoo. But if you try to tell me that you're a zoo expert or even that you have a faint understanding of what a zoo is all about because you've seen a "Z," well, I'm sorry, I will have no choice but to argue. Vehemently.

That's probably my best description for this experiment—a vehement argument against the concept of fear. In this experiment, you'll learn that we really do love each other. As Barack Obama, senator from Illinois, said in a recent interview with Oprah, we all have so much more in common than we have differences.

The Human Genome Project, a huge international research project that took 13 years, mapped out human DNA. People were a little concerned at first, because they worried we'd use the results against certain people.

Furthermore, the Genome Project found out that humans are 99.99 percent the same.

Of all the millions of genes that make up our genetic code, the things that make us different amounts to less than one percent of one percent.

Don't you get it? We are all the same. We all age and lose our hair the same way. We're all susceptible to the same diseases and treated by the same cures. We all make love and reproduce, and feel things in the exact same way. How could we possibly think the letter "z" is the whole picture?

ANECDOTAL EVIDENCE

"Ultimately, I think people are more afraid of love than they are of terrorism."
—Ian Rhett

Best-selling author Martha Beck was once like most of us. Friendly enough, trusting enough, but not about to go overboard. After all, she was a scientist, a Harvard-pedigreed sociologist who needed facts to form any kind of conclusion. And the conclusion she came to, the same one most all of us come to on planet earth, is that people are okay, but you don't want to get too involved. Especially not if you're at Harvard and trying to get your second graduate degree. Probably best to keep people at arm's distance.

As she describes it in her wonderful book, *Expecting Adam*, "We go around like Queen Elizabeth, bless her heart, clutching our dowdy little accessories, avoiding the slightest hint of impropriety, never showing our real feelings or touching anyone else except through glove leather."

But Cosmo K in Its infinitely good humor pulled a fast one on Martha Beck. It gave her a Downs Syndrome son (Adam) who taught her that everything she thought she understood about the world is a big ruse. Especially the part about not trusting other people. When she was pregnant with Adam, her husband, also a Harvard graduate student, traveled to Asia a lot, and she was left at home to cope with her demanding studies, the couple's two-year-old, and the pregnancy that was not going well. Fires, potential miscarriages, and ongoing pregnancy ailments drove her to wit's end.

As she says, "I felt like a load of gravel had been dumped on me."

But every time she was about to snap, an angel (and I don't mean metaphorically) or an acquaintance she barely knew would show up with kind words, groceries, or some other assistance she needed at all times. Keep in mind that this is a woman who had to be on the edge of desperation for anything like this to get through. She had long ago eschewed any notion of God and was sworn by education to follow the good old Baconian logic of refusing to believe anything until proven true.

Nonetheless, a woman she barely knew showed up on her doorstep with groceries one morning when she was about to pass out, an unseen force appeared out of nowhere to guide her through her smoke-filled apartment when it burned to the ground, and she was able to see and talk to her husband even though he was in Hong Kong and she was in Boston. And, no, I don't mean by telephone.

What she came to realize is that "Against all odds, despite everything that works against it on this unpleasant, uncomfortable planet, mothering is here in abundance. You can always find it, if you're smart enough and know where to look." Even if you aren't smart enough it tends to show up—especially if you really need it.

Says Beck: "I have had to jettison every sorrow, every terror, every misconception, every lie that stands between my conscious mind and what I've come to know in my heart to be true. I have been forced to expand reality from a string of solid facts, as narrow and cold as a razor's edge to a wild chaos of possibility."

THE METHOD:

"You cannot really be stranded in a Universe that is so accommodating."
—Eric Butterworth

Materials needed: One extra-large stuffed animal, at least three-feet tall. The persuasion of stuffed animal is unimportant. Goofier, the better. When I tried the experiment, I carried a big brown moose my daughter calls Moosletoe and occasionally sleeps with. I brought it to her from Montana when I was up there working on a cattle ranch.

How to proceed: Wherever you go for the next 48 hours—to the office, the grocery store, the opera—carry the giant stuffed animal.

Pay attention to the reaction of the people you see. See if any of the following preconceived notions hold up.

"People are stuck up and keep to themselves."

"People are preoccupied with their own problems."

"It's important to be dignified and act like a mature grownup."

"People aren't really that friendly. Or maybe they are, but they certainly don't talk to me."

LAB REPORT SHEET

The Principle:
The Harry Houdini Principle

The Theory:
Everything that doesn't look like love is smoke and mirrors.

The Question:
Is it possible that people are really good and that it's only my illusions that keeping me from noticing?

Hypothesis:
If I put myself out there in a bold, goofy way, people will love me.

Time required:
48 hours

Today's Date:

Time:

The Approach:
Well, all I can say to this principle, God, is you obviously have never met my Aunt Sally. Or worked a day underneath my boss. I'm starting to buy this business about you being cool and all, but there is no way I'm buying it about everybody else.

Research Notes:

Research Notes Continued:

EXPERIMENT # 10:

THE CHEESE DOES NOT STAND ALONE

Everything I give is given to myself.

"You who could give the Love of God to everything you see and touch and remember are literally denying Heaven to yourself."

—Course In Miracles

PREMISE:

It's a pretty good thing we've got the spiritual world to fall back on, because the material world is looking pretty shaky these days. Between terrorists, new strains of influenza, and gaping political divides, it's pretty hard not to notice that fear is rearing its ugly head.

People are plain terrified. Which is bad enough, but fear has a tendency to distort perceptions. Severely distort them. And since we now know we can find whatever we look for, suffice it to say it's going to get worse before it gets better.

Unless. Unless, we actively decide to perceive things in a different way. I know choosing to see love when everything looks bleak is difficult and counterintuitive. But here's why it's important. It generates love.

You, average human sitting there in your easy chair, actually have the capability to create energy—not just any energy, mind you, but the most potent energy force in the world. And you can pull this potent energy at any time from thin air.

Maybe I should repeat that. You are capable of generating love. You have the ability to create love out of nothing. And with this love you can transform things that on the surface look hopeless.

And here's the even better part. Unlike fossil fuel that is unarguably running out, the love you're capable of generating will never run out. Your supply is full and running over. In fact, the more you give, the more you create. Talk about a win-win situation. When you give love unconditionally with no expectations of return, you make more love. Love, by its very nature, is abundant.

As you know, everything in the material world—from numbers to oil to black leather jackets—is limited. The material world is based on scarcity. There's not enough. You give something away, it's gone. You lose. Sorry about that, Chief!

Spiritual law states that the more we give—whether patience, tolerance, understanding or Wuyi Rock Tea—the more we get back. Give away joy, peace or anything with real value, and you'll automatically get more. That's certainly as dependable as gravity.

I know it makes no mathematical sense, but it's true and in this experiment, we'll prove it.

WHAT THE WORLD NEEDS NOW

"Mr. Gorbachev, tear down that wall."
—Ronald Reagan

Never before has the world needed more love. People today feel cut-off, isolated, fragmented, and alone. Even those in committed relationships can relate to the term, "love/hate." Give me what I want, I love you. Withhold what I want, you're screwed.

The bad news, of course, is you have no control over other people. The good news is you have complete and total control of how you perceive other people which, you'll learn in this experiment, can radically change your world.

Of course, you're going to have to give an old karate chop to the bricks of what you now believe. But to convince you that it might be worth it—I pose just one question. Is what you're doing now, is the way you look at life now, making you happy?

Just as I thought.

The good thing about this experiment is you don't have to leave your easy chair. The majority of your interactions with other humans occur in the nonphysical realm. All those thoughts you think you're privately keeping to yourself? They're not really private. Since we're all connected, you might as well be bellowing them over an intercom. Subtly, everyone is getting it anyway.

We're all connected to this huge data bank and we constantly exchange energy. When you generate uplifting thoughts about someone, it contributes favorably to their energy. Likewise, when you judge someone, even if you keep it to yourself, you affect their energy and the quality of your interactions. You are constantly exchanging energy with everyone in your circle of influence, and in smaller ways, with every other being on the planet.

The upside of being connected to everybody and everything is you can't really be alone. The downside, of course, is that creep you secretly hate sees past the big smile and the "yes, sir" you give him on the outside.

On some level, he knows. He can feel it. Your antagonism creates more dissension between the two of you.

Forget therapy. You can save all kinds of cash by simply changing the dialog within your own mind.

I compare the big web of life to the internet's Google search engine. Whatever you want to connect to is yours for the asking. For example, if you want to find out the names of Henry the VIII's six wives, you simply type in "wives" and Henry, the VIII and, within seconds, you get 20,000 or so hits. If you want to know how peanut butter is made, you just type in "How is peanut butter made?" and in 0.35 seconds (that's how long it took my broadband connection to made contact), you get answers from the Australian Peanut Butter Company, Peanutbutterlovers.com, and a history site that informs you that Dr. Ambrose Straub of St. Louis patented a peanut butter-making machine in 1903.

Like your computer that is hooked up to all this information, you—by virtue of being a human being—are hooked up to everyone else in the world.

You can change your world by lasering love, blessings, peace, and other high-frequency emotions to the cast of characters in your world. You're not responsible for say, Susan Sarandon, although I personally have lots of compliments and respect and love I could send her way.

Speaking of Susan Sarandon, you will probably have to act for awhile. Doesn't matter if you've never taken acting lessons. I know for a fact that when you were a kid you were awesome at "make believe." That's all you have to do.

First role. Mother Teresa. Remember how that little 5'2" woman with the wrinkly face just oozed love? From what I hear, just being in her presence could alter your DNA. Well, pretend you are her. Or someone like her. Pretend that you are someone who has so much love, compassion, and tenderness that people flock to your door. Pretend that you have no judgments, that nothing bothers you and that your life goal includes giving as much as you can.

Okay, got it? Next role. Luke Skywalker. Well actually, Mother Teresa as Luke Skywalker. You're still this loving, potent force for good, only now you're in your spaceship shooting all these beneficient thoughts out to the people in your world.

Since you're connected to everyone and everything, it's quite likely these people will actually feel your bolts of good blessings, but that's not why you're doing it. You're doing it because you will (if you're doing this right) come up with two conclusions. A) Sending out love makes you feel pretty good and B) The more you send out, the more you get back.

As it says in the Course, "You are being blessed by every beneficient thought of any of your brothers anywhere."

A protester was standing outside the Military School of America, protesting the policies of the United States and its bully behavior. Someone asked him, "What makes you think holding that little candle is going to have any effect on these governments? They've been doing what they do for decades now."

He said, "I'm not worried about changing them. I don't want my country to change me."

ANECDOTAL EVIDENCE:

> "All we want, whether we are honeybees, ponderosa pines, coyotes, human beings, or stars, is to love and be loved, to be accepted, cherished and celebrated simply for being who we are. Is that so very difficult?"
>
> —Derrick Jensen

My friend who I'll call Ginger because that's not her name had a rocky relationship with her mother for years. Finally, she decided that every night before falling asleep she would send her mom blessings. Her mom, of course, had no idea she was doing this. To this day, Ginger has never told her mother that for six months, she spent a few minutes each evening envisioning her getting all the things she ever wanted and seeing herself being happy about it.

"I honestly don't know how it happened, but our relationship changed. Now, we're the best of friends," Ginger says.

METHOD:

> "We can slice and dice it anyway we like, but we cannot justify turning our face away from this evidence."
>
> —Larry Dossey

In 1972, at the annual convention of the American Association for the Advancement of Science, a meteorologist named Edward Lorenz introduced a brand new term into the

American vernacular. The "butterfly effect" was his observation that an event as seemingly insignificant as the flapping of a butterfly's wings in Brazil could set off a hurricane in Texas. In other words, small, almost imperceptible things can have large and momentous consequences.

That's what this experiment is about. By something as seemingly insignificant as changing your thoughts about someone you dislike, you can alter history.

Is it really possible in this us vs. them world that we, as spiritual principle states, are really one?

Well, to be blunt . . . yeah. We're all in this together. And every time we judge or think anything less than charitable about anyone, we crucify ourselves. We literally inflict self-pain.

Our differences, as huge as we make them out to be, are superficial and meaningless. And it's time we let them go.

When you meet anyone, remember it is a holy encounter. As you see him you will see yourself. As you treat him, you will treat yourself. As you think of him you will think of yourself.

This, my friend, is power.

You can literally change your relationships with anyone by simply sending them good thoughts.

Think of the person you most despise. You can't fool me. I know someone has popped into your head. For the sake of the experiment, it's best to choose someone you talk to on a regular basis. Someone you can comfortably call at the end of the 48-hour experiment.

Okay, now, for the next 48 hours, as hard as this might be, you're going to think of every good thought you can about this person. You're going to send them incomparable blessings. You're going to think about them winning the lottery, getting a date with Brad Pitt, winning a trip around the world on the QE2.

If you must, go back to a time they were still a sweet, little boo-boo in a pink or blue baby bonnet. If you must, use the prayer a friend of mine used when his best friend began dating his ex-wife. When I first suggested he might want to forgive the guy (again, for his own peace of mind, not because the guy necessarily deserved it), he said, "There is no way." That was No Way with a capital "N" and a capital "W." But he did agree to an experiment.

This is what he'd say. "If a truck doesn't run over you first, I wish you health, prosperity, and a good life." After four or five days, he dropped the truck line and within a month, they were best friends again. And he went on to marry a woman with whom he has a five times better relationship than that with his ex-wife.

LAB REPORT SHEET

The Principle:
The cheese does not stand alone.

The Theory:
Everything I give is given to myself.

The Question:
Can I change my interactions with those around me by perceiving them differently?

Hypothesis:
If for 48 hours, I spend time giving out love, my perception of the world will change.

Time required:
48 hours

Today's Date:

Time:

Research Notes:

YOU AND ME AGAINST THE MATERIAL WORLD

"You are doing this because you are fantastic and brave and curious. And, yes, you are probably a little crazy. And this is a good thing."

—Chris Baty

High-fives! You made it through the book, and hopefully through the ten experiments. You've bravely cast your hat into the ring. That means the hardest part is over. But if you quit now, you miss the best part of the whole adventure. This is where the payback begins.

What I'd like to suggest is that you form a circle in your home town or home church or Home Depot (although don't tell them I sent you) with other readers of *God Doesn't Have Bad Hair Days.*

Even though Cosmo K is always with us, always guiding us, sometimes it helps to have someone with a body to remind us. And heaven knows, we could use the company.

Because, quite frankly, you're going to hit a wall. You'll begin to have second thoughts. Start to fall back into your old patterns. Even though you've made the decision to seize your spiritual destiny. Even though you've seen glimpses of the available majesty, you'll start to lag in determination, to struggle to stay on task. You'll be tempted to take oh, you know, just a short little break until after you lose ten pounds or get the new tile for your guest bathroom.

That's why it's vital to find some partners in crime, some fellow spiritual warriors who are willing to listen, to cheer, and to remind you just why you're doing this.

It doesn't have to be a four-hour commitment. Maybe you'll want to do it over the phone. But it's important to enlist others who will help you keep three things in mind:

> **1.** You are awesome. Whether you realize it or not, you are a tremendously powerful spiritual being. Currents of possibilities run so deep in your bones that

you will continue to be unhappy until you finally "get it."

2. The great God of your being has big plans for you. All it takes is a little dedication. And a lot of resolve. Make mind training a daily part of your life and your life will take care of itself. Guaranteed.

3. We're all in this together. If we take care of one another, and go the extra mile to keep each other motivated and on track, we all gain. If we reach out with compassion whenever someone is struggling, we're all lifted up. Sure, we could walk alone to the finish line. But the real joy comes from tackling the journey together, from raising our voices in one mighty, unified yeehaw.

ABOUT THE AUTHOR

PAM GROUT is the author of 13 books, including *Living Big: Embrace Your Passion, Leap Into an Extraordinary Life*, and *Jumpstart Your Metabolism: With the Power of Breath*. Her articles have appeared in the *Washington Post, Outside, Travel & Leisure, Scientific American Explorations,* and many others. She is a playwright, a screenwriter, a reporter for *People* magazine, and the mother of the world's most magnificent 12-year-old. She lives in Lawrence, Kansas with Tasman, the aforementioned 12-year-old and their cat, Trivia Quantum Morpheus X-Cat, Mr. Norris Grout.